Wicked
BOZEMAN

Wicked
BOZEMAN

KELLY SUZANNE HARTMAN

with contributions by the Gallatin Historical Society
and Gallatin History Museum

THE
History
PRESS

Published by The History Press
Charleston, SC
www.historypress.com

First published 2022

ISBN 978-1-5402-5245-6

Library of Congress Control Number: 2022933369

Notice: The information in this book is true and complete to the best of our knowledge. It is offered without guarantee on the part of the author or The History Press. The author and The History Press disclaim all liability in connection with the use of this book.

CONTENTS

INTRODUCTION

This book is composed of the prison records in the collection of the Gallatin Historical Society, ranging from 1893 to 1935. Supplemental research was done in newspaper articles predating 1893 and from 1935 to 1940, to gain insight into the earliest criminal activity in the area. Using this invaluable database of names in the record books, I was often able to match the perpetrators with contemporary news articles, prison records and ancestral information. To this end, I used a variety of resources, including the wonderful collection of newspapers at the Gallatin Historical Society, digitized papers on Chronicling America and Newspapers.com, the historical society's family research files, Ancestry.com, the Montana Memory Project's prison records from the Montana Historical Society and other jail records at the Gallatin History Museum. There are many stories that are left unknown, such as those of rape and houses of ill repute, as so little of that history was recorded in these sources at the time of its occurrence.

The jail ledgers were invaluable to me as contemporary records of the passage of men and women in and out of the building. I used these as the landing point for my research, taking note of interesting people and crimes to conduct further research about. Some yielded great results, others came up frustratingly empty—and there were, perhaps, fascinating stories connected with seemingly insignificant crimes that I have missed. Out of the thousands of names listed, however, I hope that I have been able to bring a balance of interesting stories and people back to life.

Perhaps one of the most important things I took from my work on this book was the weight of time lost in incarceration. Time spent in jail or prison changed some of the prisoners' views and made them better people; it was a wake-up call of sorts. But many prisoners' crimes became repeat crimes, and one can watch their faces grow old with every intake photo. With this in mind, I kept a balance of crimes that make you laugh, such as an attorney shooting a pheasant out of season, and ones that shake you with the reality of time lost to poor decisions, as in the case of Henry Hinkley, who lost his wife and grew old in and out of prison due to his penchant for forgery.

I would like to thank the Gallatin Historical Society/Museum for letting me use their vast historic resources on this project and my curatorial assistant, Victoria Richard, whose help researching and scouring newspapers was invaluable. Thanks to her assistance, the Gallatin History Museum now has interpretive panels throughout the building that will bring to life those who spent time within its walls.

The old building still has stories to share, and as each one resurfaces, so, too, does the evidence waiting to be found in the brick and mortar, steel bars and concrete walls that make up this profoundly essential piece of history.

Chapter 1

THE JAILS OF BOZEMAN

A History of Imprisonment

A man with a good pair of shoes could kick his way out of the jail in an hour.
—*The* Republican-Courier, *November 1, 1910*

Five years following Bozeman's establishment in 1864 and two years after it became the Gallatin County seat, county commissioners felt the need for a jail. Citizens of the county were asked to build the jail, then sell it to the county in 1869. Funds were procured from investors, and a total of $487.50 was gathered up to pay for the new jail.

This first jail was labeled on an 1884 Sanborn map as the Log Calaboose and was located on South Mendenhall Street, about one hundred feet west from the Bozeman Creek. Perhaps the most startling occurrence at this oft-empty jail was the vigilante capture and execution of two prisoners, Z.A. Triplett and John W. St. Clair. The men had been locked in the jail when vigilantes broke in, pulled them out and hanged them both on a meat rack just outside the town.

In 1874, improvements were made on the building, including a new shingle roof and the addition of two cells. Later that same year, a guardroom was added, and the *Bozeman Avant Courier* boasted how secure and conveniently arranged the building was. According to the *Courier*, the jail was "one of the best in the Territory, which is due to an efficient and wide-awake Sheriff." The room was kept clean and adequately heated during the winter, and the food was as good as that in a hotel.

Train of Conestoga wagons on Main Street, Bozeman, circa 1864. *Gallatin Historical Society/ Gallatin History Museum.*

Besides the confinement and the prisoners' consciousness of the crimes they had committed, it was believed those inside had it better than many on the outside. However, this satisfaction with the facility would not last. Interestingly, in 1884, it was noted that fifty prisoners were held in jails because there was no room at the penitentiary. Clearly, crime was on the rise, and needs would rapidly change across the territory.[1]

In 1878, the town felt the need for a courthouse, and a vote soon authorized the construction of a $25,000 building with a more secure jail in the basement. Once the vote had passed, an invitation for bids was sent out to secure a location for the new building site. Surprisingly, many of the offers were "free gratis," including many desirable tracts of land near the business center of the town. Some offers even included a bonus of bricks that could be used in the building. Apparently east and west Bozeman were in a bit of a scuffle over who could secure the site, leaving many to wonder if the courthouse and jail would need to be split into two buildings instead of one, with one institution given to each side. At that time, the jail was situated in east Bozeman. It was believed that Gallatin County's founding fathers would pick the site that was best suited for the institutions and not be swayed by the offers of free land or bricks.[2]

The location was to be the corner of Main and Fourth Streets, which is roughly the same place where the current courthouse stands. The architectural plans were drawn up by Byron Vreeland, whose son Pomeroy Vreeland, also an architect, would be killed by crazed ranch hand Buford Webb on October 10, 1919. The building would not be completed until July 11, 1881, and would feature a small jail yard in the back, which was fenced in with a high brick wall with broken glass bottles embedded in its upper edge. On December 27, 1883, John A. Clark would be executed on a gallows in this jail yard, as would be Lu Sing on April 20, 1906.

A tour of the jail by the territorial grand jury in 1885 showed the building was clean and the prisoners satisfied with their treatment. Recommendations for improvement included new straw in the bedding, a new stovepipe, new whitewash in the cells and repairs to the sewerage, as it was unusable.[3] In 1887, at the close of their tour, it was found that water was running from the roof to under the building, undermining the foundation of the courthouse.[4]

It seems inmate labor was, on occasion, used to shovel snow for public places, like local schools. In fact, a rather humorous story about the jail

Gallatin County Courthouse (1881–1938) and the Clerk and Recorder's Office (1884–1908) on West Main Street. *Gallatin Historical Society/Gallatin History Museum.*

and schools came about in 1883, when a real estate agent was showing a "tenderfoot" the town, hoping to sell him some of early Bozeman founder Daniel Rouse's lots. While passing the school, the agent noted the gallows that had been built in front of it and, since it was not yet needed in the jail yard, remained in its place. The agent jokingly stated that the gallows was there to remind children of the value of education. It was no wonder, he quipped, that every man, woman and child in Montana could read and write. The tenderfoot called on the agent the following day to cancel his offer on the lots and "bid a hasty farewell to Bozeman and Montana."[5]

The *Avant Courier* and the *Weekly Chronicle* were at odds when it came to using the jail for prisoners from outside of the scope of the county. In 1884, the *Courier* believed that many cases from Cooke City and Livingston had been brought to the Gallatin County Jail with the motive of "giving employment to and paying the expenses of some deputy sheriff who desired to come to Bozeman." The paper believed that these expenses were unnecessary and were putting the county in debt. The *Weekly Chronicle* fervently disagreed, stating that "the prosecution of crime must not be condoned because it costs a few dollars." The *Chronicle* noted that the rate of crime had increased, as evidenced by the amount of convictions, which undoubtedly would increase costs for taxpayers.[6] In February 1884, there were thirty-two prisoners held at the county jail, two of which had just arrived from Livingston.[7] As a side note, a county physician was contracted to care for the sick at the poor farm and the jail and for anyone who was a charge of the county.

In August 1888, the *Bozeman Weekly Chronicle* noted that the county jail was "beyond the danger of being cut to pieces by the prisoner and his meat saw," as no one that year had been confined within its walls for longer than two weeks at a time. According to the paper, this stint of low crime took away "a great deal of Prohibitionistic thunder which is wont to be applied by the temperance orator who, in a loud voice, points to the jail and argues that the cause of crime and the overflowing jails is immediately attributable to whiskey drinking."[8]

By 1910, however, the jail was past capacity. Women, children, witnesses and minor offenders would at times be confined thirty persons to a room, without separation and without enough beds to sleep on. It was clear a new jail was needed to sustain the town's criminal population. A supplement to the *Republican-Courier* on November 1, 1910, made a plea to "Vote for New Jail." The plea addressed both health and monetary issues with the present jail, noting that "some day one of the worst contagions this section has ever seen is bound to emanate" from the building. It was said that visitors could feel the stifling effect of the air when stepping into the building, and there was concern for the county officials who had to spend hours each day in "such a vile smelling place." The health concerns carried over into the monetary situation in the county. It was, at that time, illegal for prisoners to be held in a basement apartment, which is exactly what the current jail was. If a prisoner became ill due to the conditions in this place, a lawsuit could ensue, which could cost the taxpayers of the county heavily. It was also noted that the sheriff would be hard-pressed to keep desperate criminals in the jail, as "a man with a good pair of shoes could kick his way out of the jail in an hour."[9]

A bond would be promoted and pass, and this time, local architect Fred Willson was the designer, with a budget of $35,000. He would come in under at $33,932.49. The second-largest expense was the contract for the steel cell work, which cost $8,461. The Diebold Pipe and Lock Company was contracted for the cells, vault and gallows mechanism. On December 2, 1911, the new jail officially opened for business; the construction of the new building took only about half a year.[10]

When plans for the building were officially submitted in March 1911, the *Republican-Courier* announced that the bastille would be second to none in Montana and that it would be "unusually handsome…and so attractive both inside and out that vagrants and petty criminals instead of trying to

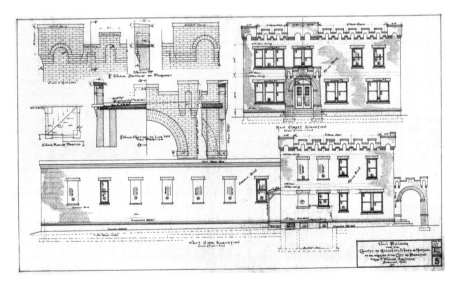

Jail building exterior drawings by Fred Willson, architect, 1911. *Gallatin Historical Society/ Gallatin History Museum.*

break out of jail, will want to break in during the winter months." There was only to be one entrance to this jail; the vestibule would open on the deputy's office to the right and the dining room to the left. When the housing was occupied by a married sheriff, his wife would cook for the prisoners. A food pass-through was built into the jail building, which allowed food from the kitchen to be handed to a jailer through a small hole in the wall. When the building first opened for "business," it was noted that even should the cells overflow, there was room for a second tier of cells to be placed on top of the current ones. The jail could hold fifty prisoners at a time easily, but the space could be utilized to hold seventy-five, if needed. The sheriff would have a private office, and beyond the deputy's office would lie the jailer's office, followed by the jail. It was believed then that one jailer could maintain the building, as any prisoner attempting escape would have to pass through the jailer's office.[11] However, on December 22, 1911, it was discovered that six prisoners had indeed escaped this brand-new "escape proof" building.

This building would preside as the jail for over seventy years, seeing many a successful and attempted escape and the execution of Seth Danner, the only man who ever stood on the Diebold Company's gallows (look for *Murder along the Yellowstone Trail: The Execution of Seth Danner* for more). But a new jail

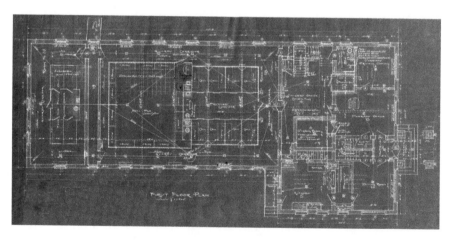

Above: Blueprint of the jail by Fred Willson, 1910. *Gallatin Historical Society/Gallatin History Museum.*

Opposite, top: Gallatin Historical Society members and Gallatin county commissioners gathered for the signing of documents establishing the Pioneer Museum in the former Gallatin County Jail. *Gallatin Historical Society/Gallatin History Museum.*

Opposite, bottom: The Gallatin History Museum, located in the old Gallatin County Jail building. *Author's image.*

Left: Original key box in the jailer's office of the 1911 jail; the "insane" key is missing. *Author's image.*

Below: Present-day photo of Siberia (the isolation cells), where the insane were often kept. *Image by Victoria Richard.*

by-fifty-two-foot, two-story building with brick veneering.[15] According to the *New North-West*, Deer Lodge's newspaper, the need for an asylum was of a "measure of humanity and economy."[16]

One story of insanity began as a search for gold. In 1883, Jack Nye, while prospecting in the Big Hole area, believed he had found the "lost cabin lode." Bozeman reporters, wiring the news to the *Minneapolis Journal* in expectant hope and curiosity, told the story of the mysterious mother lode. According to the *Weekly Chronicle*, some years prior, a group of miners had discovered the richest "body of quartz in the known world," somewhere near the Big Horn River. On their way down the mountain in a homemade boat, on a mission to gather more supplies and men, they were attacked by Native Americans. Only one of the three escaped, but he reached town in a bad way. The lone survivor was unwilling to tell of the exact location of the lode and became insane over his "constant pondering over this immense mine of wealth." It was not reported if Jack Nye had indeed found this lost treasure, but the story breathes old West mystery and discovery.[17]

It was determined at the fifteenth legislature that each inmate of an asylum was to have one postal contact outside of the hospital with whom they could always correspond, a right that allowed for transparency in the event that a person was cured but could not escape those who ran the institution. It was also noted that each person leaving the asylum was to be given a set of clothing and twenty dollars in cash with which to start their lives again.[18] While given something to begin anew, some lost all when committed, such as John G. Stevens, noted "Insane Person," whose mining claims in the New World Mining District at Cooke City were sold in a sheriff's sale by his guardians.[19] On May 23 of the following year, 1887, Stevens died at the Warm Springs hospital.[20]

Just two years prior to Stevens's death, a tragedy occurred at Warm Springs when a fire broke out in the asylum. The *Chronicle* does not list the men who died, nor how many, but it appears it was more than one. Those running the institution escaped any blame by the coroner's jury.[21]

An opinion-based article in the *Bozeman Avant Courier* on July 4, 1878, discussed the causes of insanity. According to the article, "Insanity was not common among the native Indians of our country, but it prevails to an alarming extent in New England civilization." The author of the article believed that the recent civil war had devalued currency and led to dishonesty in the insurance companies and banking institutions. This, in turn, created financial disturbances that increased a lack of reasoning in persons, leading to either insanity or suicide: "There is scarcely a daily paper issued but what contains an account of an insane person being taken to a lunatic asylum or a man or woman who has committed suicide with the comment—financial troubles was the only apparent cause!" The author stated the idea, a common one at the time, that the mind is never diseased; disease can only affect the organs. Therefore, it is the brain that is affected when these outside influences arise. It was inferred that the mind and the brain were separate, and in order to cure a disturbed mind, the organ of the brain must be dealt with. While understanding of the mind and the causes of mental distress have been further studied since this point in time, it is still relevant to consider how much financial stress leads to mental stress.[22]

Jailer's key box; the key for the isolation cells marked "insane" is missing. *Author's image.*

A similar article appeared in the same paper in December 1879, written by W.B. Cary, titled "Why Farmer's Wives Become Insane." In it, the author writes about a farmer's daughter who, after a respite back East, returned to the farm with "rosy cheeks, and fresh, elastic manners," only to be found at the end of the summer shockingly worn and tired in the face. The author questions why nobody saw that the girl was overworked and worried. Cary notes that, in a recent report on insane asylums, farmer's wives and daughters made up the largest proportion of female inmates. To explain this phenomenon, Cary looks at the workload of a woman on the farm versus that of the man:

The man has a constant change of scene with all the excitement…he goes from breakfast to the plow, the harrow and the constantly-varying duties of the farm. He come[s] to dinner—and to supper prepared for him and after supper goes out to the barn or the neighbor's dooryard to smoke a comfortable pipe and chat with the neighbors about the crops. The wife rises to kindle the fire, dress the children, cook breakfast, wash the dishes, send the children to school, get dinner, wash the dishes,—and if there is a moment to spare between dinner and supper, to spend it in sewing,—get supper, wash dishes, put the children to bed,—and if a moment more offers, to sew, besides taking care of the morning and evening milk, gathering eggs, churning and

*working butter, and a hundred things that must be done every day, in exactly
the same way and order,—and then, perhaps, meet the sour or disappointed
looks of the lord of the manor if anything is amiss in all this endless detail
of drudgery.*[23]

How to solve such a cycle of drudgery? According to Cary, the best
medicine would be for farmers to provide recreation for their wives and
daughters, to take them on rides in the wagon often to break up the monotony
of their lives. The farmer's daughter Cary knew may have benefited from
this remedy, but most would say more changes would probably have been
needed to change the trajectory of the girl's health. Another article titled
"Variety," published in May 1878, also concludes that "sameness is the
border-land of insanity."[24]

As with most diseases of the day, there were also those cure-all drugs
that may have done the trick. One such, Murry's Specific, a "Great English
Remedy," supposedly could cure the symptoms—like weak memory,
headache, pain in the back, wakefulness, etc.—that often led to insanity.[25]
One can guess how effective these remedies were. In 1878, the *Courier* noted
that insanity was on the rise in the United States, particularly in California.
According to recent statistics, there was one insane person for every 160
people in California and one for every 343 in the United States on average.
This was compared to one in 440 in the entire country of France.[26] One
can see why Montanans were concerned about the care of those among
them who needed extra help. According to the *Anaconda Review* in 1885, the
asylum at Warm Springs, however, provided excellent care. Dr. Mussigbrod
was commended for gladdening the inmates with presents suited for each,
which, that year alone, were valued at $600 among them all. It was noted
that "each time he enters a compartment where patient[s] are kept they vie
with each other in being first to grasp his hand and endeavor in every way to
show feelings of love and respect."[27]

The November 18, 1885 edition of the *Bozeman Weekly Chronicle* contained
a fascinating article about a Charles Henry Blackwell, who lodged at a room
at the Northern Pacific Hotel. After a few days, the chambermaid went to
his room to find the lodger hanging by the neck. However, what she saw
was not reality. With investigation, it was discovered the "body" was only
Blackwell's clothes, stuffed to look like a man hanging from a nail, with his
name labeled on the effigy. The sheriff rounded up the real Blackwell, and it
was soon determined by committee that the man was insane; it was assumed
that he would thence be sent to the Territorial Insane Asylum.[28] That same

The Guy House circa 1870, which later became the Northern Pacific Hotel. *Gallatin Historical Society/Gallatin History Museum.*

year, the state legislature was looking for a location for a bigger government-run asylum. The *Chronicle* touted Dr. Hunter's Hot Springs as the perfect location because of its location near the railroad and the healing qualities of the waters in that vicinity.[29]

In 1886, John Hallenhan released a bald eagle that belonged to Cy Mounts and began to pray before the bird, worshipping it as an idol. He was soon taken to Warm Springs.[30] However, not all were taken to the insane asylum, as some were not deemed clinically insane by committee. Often, these cases were sent to the poor farm, as was Mrs. Miner, whose husband's complaint was the cause of her coming before a committee.[31] The poor farm was judged by a committee to be in excellent condition; however, the local jail was found to be lacking. It was noted that the space was too small for the seclusion of women, children or the insane from the other prisoners. That May, it was reported there were 138 patients at Warm Springs, eighteen of them being women.[32]

Nelson and Ellen Story, early Bozeman pioneers, had a brush with insanity in December 1886 when an Owen J. McCann arrived at their home. Nelson had received two notes from the man, one a postcard simply bearing Owen's name and one a letter of unknown content. When Owen arrived, Nelson was not at home; regardless, the man asked to see their daughter. Mrs. Story refused and told the man to be gone. Soon after, Nelson received a letter of apology from Owen, which he in turn replied to. This interaction did little to deter the man, who again arrived at the home. When asked what he wanted, the man stated, "I am Owen McCann. I have taken a liking to your daughter," to which he was cut short and knocked down by Nelson. Owen quickly pulled a bulldog revolver but was fired upon by Ellen with a shotgun from where she stood at the door, to no effect. Nelson attempted to shoot as well, but his gun was unable to go off, and Owen left. He was soon arrested, and it was noted that many in the town had considered the man insane.[33] The case came up before the Supreme Court of Montana in Helena in January 1887. Following a brief stint at Warm Springs, Owen was released, and his case was discharged at the hearing in Helena due to the

Studio portrait of Ellen Story. *Gallatin Historical Society/Gallatin History Museum.*

unconstitutionality of the laws for insanity. It was noted the law was not "according to due process of law, as it permits any man to be deprived of his liberty upon the verdict of three jurymen, all of whom are peremptorily summoned by the probate judge."[34] Insanity was often exhibited over unrequited love. David Stratton of Bear Gulch was arrested for becoming too enamored with a woman who did not reciprocate. When turned down, he went insane.

In 1887, it was proposed that the site of the Fort Ellis military reservation and buildings be donated to the territory for an insane hospital. The proposal was only partially supported and sent to a special committee.[35] It had been noted that if Gallatin County wanted the asylum, they could procure it, but it seems the idea was not pushed through to fruition. Before the creation of a state asylum, those who needed care were distributed among private individuals under contract. This, of course, led to abuse of the contract, to the detriment of the patients. It was of regional importance to establish a government institution. It was believed that before another year passed, "the manner in which Montana cares for those who are unable to provide for themselves should rebound to her credit instead of to her disgrace."[36] It seems places in Wisconsin had adopted methods of caring for the insane by becoming more personal with the patients and allowing them more room to be at liberty. The idea was appealing to those in Montana who were interested in caring for those among them who could not care for themselves.

Ledger book containing orders that confirmed people to the insane asylum, detailing their hearings and transfers to Warm Springs, 1896–1929. *Gallatin Historical Society/Gallatin History Museum.*

There were also, in turn, many suicides that mention insanity as the cause of the person's death. On May 9, 1883, it was reported that David Brown had shot himself in his cabin on the West Gallatin. He was found with a calmly written note on his person that stated his name, date of birth and hometown of Dundee, Scotland. It was determined that insanity was the cause through the testimony of those who knew the man, like his foreman at a ditch, Mr. Schmaker, who stated that, in conversations with Brown, he had detected insanity. Brown was only twenty-one years old.[37] Another case of suicide occurred in 1886 in the old Bozeman jail. George S. Budd was awaiting his journey to Warm Springs when he got hold of a razor and cut his own throat before it could be taken from him. Within two hours, he had died from internal bleeding. George was twenty-five years old.[38]

Perhaps the strangest story to be told related to insanity is that of Jesse Anderson. In 1910, Deputy Sheriff Dan Kilbride stumbled upon a heavily armed man near Spring Hill Creek. When approached, the man threatened Kilbride (who was unarmed at the time). By the time Kilbride could make a return trip more equipped, the "bird had flown." The next day, however, a report came in from a ranch near Belgrade that an armed man had demanded food at gunpoint. With this new information, the man was soon found, asleep with his finger on the trigger of his cocked gun. He came along easily, thinking that the officers knew what was up; little did he know that they had no clue who he was. At the jail, his description—five foot three inches tall, 139 pounds, bowlegged, thirty-eight years old with a dark complexion—was matched to that of Jesse Anderson, alias Albert Ross, an escapee of the mental institution at Warm Springs. He had escaped a year earlier and hadn't been caught, until now.[39]

But the story gets even stranger. When he was booked, it was discovered that the man had on a "half corset of steel ribs of his own make." In fact, he also had steel plates at his forearms and the crown of his cap, all, presumably, bulletproof. A photograph was taken of Anderson standing in

Homemade bulletproof cap and vest made by Jesse Anderson. *Author's image.*

front of the original Gallatin County Courthouse by Schlechten Studio, and a wonderful newspaper article followed, which noted that "his steel armor will make a valuable addition to the collection of curios in the sheriff's office."[40] Escapes of this nature seem to have happened often. In 1923, an escaped inmate was found on the Green Ranch at Willow Creek and returned to the hospital.[41]

In 1912, a sad case of disillusionment ended in the death of the man who became insane over an imaginary mortgage. It seems Fred Hopf, a rancher from the Bridger area, had been confused by a clerical error that made it appear that a mortgage of a large sum was held over the ranch that he and his wife had worked so hard to acquire. Despite attempts by his wife and friends to sway his worries, due to the mortgage having been an error and nothing more, Hopf retained the worry, and it grew in him until insanity ensued.

The examination of Hopf was recorded by the *Republican-Courier*. The paper stated that Hopf was born in Germany in 1838, immigrating to America as a baby. He had worked for others for many years before getting married in 1897. When his wife and ten-year-old daughter entered the examination room, the incoherent man lit up, kissing them both. His wife

WORRY OVER AN IMAGINARY MORTGAGE CAUSES INSANITY

One of Life's Pathetic Features Revealed in Office of Sheriff When Fred Hopf was Examined for Insanity— Pitiful Story Related by Wife

Opposite: Postcard of Jesse Anderson standing in front of the old Gallatin County Courthouse, taken by Schlechten Studio. *Gallatin Historical Society/Gallatin History Museum.*

Above: *Republican-Courier*, January 30, 1912. *Gallatin Historical Society/Gallatin History Museum.*

told their story, which had involved years of hard work to bring their debt down to $200. A clerical error nearly undid all their hard work, but it was discovered and easily remedied. Hopf did not, or could not, understand the error nor how it had been fixed, and so the slip into insanity began. According to the paper, the error had been a mistake in the direction of a lot of land, but to Hopf, it seemed like a conspiracy to rob him of his land. The idea preyed at his mind, until he could not eat or sleep. First, physicians were called for, then he was brought to stay in the padded cell of the jail, and finally, he was to be sent to Warm Springs for a spell.[42]

The error had been discovered in July 1911, prior to which Hopf had not had any behavioral issues. The downhill spiral of his mind happened fast. According to the *Anaconda Standard* of January 30, 1912, the man had to be bound while on the train to Warm Springs. The doctors who examined him stated it was one of the most violent cases they had come across. Sadly, Fred Hopf would pass away at the asylum just two weeks after his arrival. The cause of death was not stated, but it is supposed he had been worn down by so much worry. The *Republican-Courier* noted that he left "a rock covered farm, a little stock, as property to his wife and two children"—land that they could have survived on, the way they had in the fifteen years prior, had the clerical error not proved to be fatal.[43]

In a 1918 report (republished in 1923), it was determined that 21.1 percent of the male cases in the state hospital were due to alcoholism. According to the 1923 report, Prohibition had lowered this to less than 5

those who were "feeble minded" or had criminal records. Indeed, the only man executed in the Gallatin County Jail, Seth Orrin Danner, was considered as a test subject for the bill. According to Dr. John Neuman, who was associated with the State University in Missoula at the time, "life comes from pre-existing life," and consequently, a person of "feeble mind" would produce offspring of a similar nature. It was noted that, in 1923 alone, there had been 1,865 applicants for Montana state institutions for the insane, while the capacity limit had been only 335. The cost for each inmate per year was $365, or $1 per person per day.[47] In a county report from 1924, one can see that conveyance of the insane to Warm Springs had cost the Sheriff's Department $17.87.[48] In 1925, the cost would be considerably higher at $73.39, and in 1926, it would go up again to $114.52. Under the reign of Governor Dixon in the early 1920s, the asylum's maintenance cost had been cut in half, from $652,000 to $347,000.[49]

A major case came to light in 1926 involving a Mrs. Gina Kelly versus Dr. R.J. Hathaway, superintendent of the state hospital, and Susan Kipp, a nurse. Kelly accused them of having unlawfully held her at the institution and of having performed surgical operations upon her person without her consent. This seems to have brought the hospital into everyone's consciousness, but it is likely little changed at the institution following this suit. Kelly did, in fact, win her case and was awarded $8,000.

In January 1926, James Baker, an employee of Andrew Burkenpas, was taken into custody after he attacked Burkenpas with a shovel and a knife. Justice Axtell announced that Baker would not be held for third-degree assault, allowed to pay a fine and live among the public again. According to Justice Axtell, "If Baker is unfit to be at large here he is not fit to be at large in any community. He should, if mentally unbalanced, be placed where he cannot harm others."[50]

Of note in the jail record books are the repeat offenders. There are those who were given a chance to live among their relatives, until it became clear the situation was beyond their control, and those who managed to escape the Warm Springs State Hospital, often called "the asylum." One such case of the latter involved an Al Kaufman, who had been sent to the hospital in 1922 from Bozeman. A year later, Kaufman was discovered back in Bozeman and was quickly carted back to prevent him from being a danger to others and himself.[51] In 1924, Kaufman was again apprehended and, this time, released and "floated." It is unclear what the term "floated" denoted, but it can be inferred that they probably sent him out of the county to cause trouble elsewhere.

Isolation cell in Siberia. *Author's image.*

The early morning hours of July 18, 1924, were a dark time at the Gallatin County Jail. At 2:19, Seth Orrin Danner was executed for the murder of a couple four years earlier. During those same hours, a man named Charles White, held in the presentencing cells of the jail, only steps from the gallows, killed himself. White had been brought in the day before Seth's execution

Left: View from the top of the gallows where Seth Danner was executed on July 18, 1924. Within hours, Charles White was found dead in his cell. *Author's image.*

Below: Presentencing cells. *Author's image.*

and booked as "crazy." With the department tense about the upcoming execution and the isolation cells unusable because they were occupied by Seth Danner, White was placed in a presentencing cell. Almost immediately after arriving, the man requested a doctor, saying that he had pains in his head and that he needed an operation immediately. A doctor was called for, probably mostly so that the department could remain in peace. Nothing could be done for White, who was deemed by all to be insane. He remained in the cell he had been placed in without further considerations. The two other prisoners at the jail were so unsettled by the execution that when they heard odd noises coming from the cell of Charles White, whom they could not see, they said nothing. It would not be until six o'clock on Saturday morning, just four hours following the death of Seth Danner, that Charles White would be found dead in his cell. The bed in the cell, where the man had tried to end his life by cutting his own throat, was soaked in blood. This did not accomplish the task, or maybe not fast enough, so White had then tied his belt around the bars at the top of his bed and dropped to his knees, essentially hanging himself. He had broken his own watch crystal to use the pieces as a knife. Both the watch and the belt should have been taken from the man when he was booked as "crazy." It is probable that these two items had been overlooked due to the excitement of Seth's pending execution. Little was ever known about White, other than the fact that he had been a laborer, was born in Butte and that his father resided in Plaines, Kansas.[52]

Chapter 3

DRUNK AND DISORDERLY

The Era of Prohibition

That the average distiller of the average moonshine product can drink his own liquor after knowing the filth of which the fermenting mash is composed, seems almost an impossibility.
—*The* Bozeman Courier, *January 9, 1924*

On April 21, 1923, Seth Orrin Danner and S.L. Seagraves of the Three Forks area were picked up by Constable Kaiser and Deputy Sheriff Pierce Elmore on a possession of moonshine charge. Seagraves pleaded guilty and was fined $150 by Judge Law. As many know, for Seth, this incident began the fight for his life. He would also be charged with grand larceny when stolen items were found at his home and with nonsupport of his family. Within months, Seth's wife would accuse her husband of murdering a couple they had been traveling with, and within a year Seth would be the only man executed at the Gallatin County Jail. But Seth's is another story.

Seagraves was a repeat offender, having been booked for moonshine on multiple occasions already. The fines were steep—so much, in fact, that Seagraves ended up serving the jail time instead of paying up. Out of all the crimes in the record books, those related to drunkenness, moonshine making and alcohol possession would be those with the most repeat offenders.

Montana voters approved the statewide prohibition of alcohol in November 1916; laws were put into action in December 1918, two years before the national Prohibition laws took hold. This was due, in a large part, to the efforts made by the Woman's Christian Temperance Union. Montana would also be early in its repeal of the antiliquor laws, being the first state to vote for an end to Prohibition in 1926. Nationally, Prohibition would be repealed in 1933.

From 1919 to 1926, over 250 persons were arrested for Prohibition violations in Gallatin County. Violations included possession, selling, manufacturing and the transportation of moonshine or intoxicating liquors. There were also many arrested for being drunk and disorderly, which usually led to a $10 fine and a night in jail to sleep it off. Any of the aforementioned violations, however, carried a much steeper fine. Possession most often constituted a $100–$150 fine, while the manufacture, selling or transportation of moonshine could bring about a $300–$900 fine and jail time of three to six months in most cases. Most of the offenders were men, with fewer than five women jailed during this time for Prohibition violations.

Gallatin County sheriff James Smith came into office late in 1922. During his campaign, it had apparently been circulated that he both sent moonshine to threshing crews for votes and had been continually intoxicated during the seven years he had lived in Bozeman. This rumor led Smith to place a statement in the *Bozeman Avant Courier*: "I believe in a dry town and county. I believe in enforcing the laws of the state, not as they might be interpreted, but as they are written. If elected to the office of sheriff I will use every effort in my power to suppress the moonshining and bootlegging that may be going on in Gallatin County."[53]

And he was as good as his word. During the next few years, the department, under the guidance of Sheriff Smith, would conduct a number of major raids to catch those in the act of making moonshine. Some finds, however, would be accidental, as was the case on the night of April 24, when a speeding car was stopped by the sheriff's force. In the car were Claude Solt and Charles Smith, along with forty gallons of moonshine. Both men were arrested for possession and transportation of liquor. Solt would spend forty days in jail and pay a $200 fine; Charles Smith, however, was released after eighteen days, discharged by Judge Law for a lack of evidence. A fine could be served out in a $2-a-day stay at the Gallatin County Jail.[54]

James Smith, Gallatin County sheriff from 1923 to 1927. *Gallatin Historical Society/Gallatin History Museum.*

In most instances, the confiscated moonshine was brought to the jail to be used as evidence in the arrestee's trial. In this instance, however, the forty gallons of contraband taken from the car was poured down a manhole near the courthouse. It was noted that a "thirsty crowd" watched the scene and that "scarcely had the officers finished their unwelcome task when two autos collided almost over the spot where the booze was destroyed." The paper posed the question: "Were the fumes that strong?"[55]

Directly underneath the article about the arrest of Solt and Smith was an article titled "Three Forks Men Had Some Moon." The men were S.L. Seagraves and S.O. Danner. And as mentioned earlier, this would be just the beginning of Danner's story.

At the first Bozeman Roundup during Sheriff Smith's reign, the force made a show of describing the event as the "cleanest in the history of all roundups." As a result of their efforts, eleven men were arrested for possession, transportation and selling of moonshine. In one instance, a seventy-five-gallon still, nineteen barrels of mash and fifty gallons of moonshine were confiscated from a local ranch. The *Bozeman Courier* was prompted to state that "Smith Takes 'Wild' Out of Roundup." Ironically, the winning horse of the bronc-riding event was named Moonshine.[56]

The County Sheriff's Department was not the only one to be working overtime to enforce the national Prohibition laws. The City Police Department was also hard at work. On March 6, 1923, city and county

Yakima Canutt being thrown from Moonshine. *Gallatin Historical Society/Gallatin History Museum.*

officials raided Ponsford Place, a soft drink stand. The place had been staked out for days, until a drunken man was picked up and questioned, and it was discovered he had obtained liquor from the stand. When the place was searched, moonshine was discovered in several fruit jars, a teakettle and on the person of Mr. Galbraith, proprietor.[57]

The manufacture of moonshine was not always a sanitary endeavor and could prove dangerous. In 1924, a man's chickens were killed after partaking of wet mash that officers dumped out in a farmyard. The *Bozeman Courier* noted, "That the average distiller of the average moonshine product can drink his own liquor after knowing the filth of which the fermenting mash is composed, seems almost an impossibility." In a raid in nearby Livingston, in Park County, the decomposing bodies of drowned mice were found in the bottom of barrel full of mash. Gallatin County doctors stated that the slightest presence of copperas (a green sulphate mineral) in the neck of a still could cause serious damage to the drinker. At the time, it was said there was a confiscated still in the basement of the county jail with enough copperas to "kill an entire regiment of moonshine drinkers." It is hard to determine just how often those manufacturing the substance succumbed to these hazards.[58]

In 1932, William L. Ford, age twenty-six, died from burns received when his twenty-five-gallon keg of moonshine exploded in front of him. The burns covered his body from the waist up, and what's worse, fumes and steam entered his lungs as well. Ford had been attempting to age the liquor with an electric device manufactured for that purpose when there was a malfunction, resulting in a spark that ignited the liquor. When the keg exploded, the liquor landed on Ford and immediately caught the man on fire. His wife attempted to put out the flames but became badly burned, although she would survive.[59]

A good number of stills and violators of the Prohibition law were found in the Logan area. In January 1924, three stills were discovered, all incomplete. The sheriff's force had been casing the area for days, hoping to catch the perpetrators, but they finally gave up the wait and destroyed several barrels and a large grouping of empty bottles with axes—which goes to show, even if one weren't caught, one could lose some good money in the discovery of an operation.[60] The department somewhat bungled another attempt when they arrived too early to the scene of a suspected moonshine manufacturer. Cornelius Klaver had not yet begun to make liquor when officers met him at his home in Belgrade. According to Cornelius, "If you had waited a few minutes longer you would have caught me in the act of making it. The reason I was delayed was because the fellow I got the still from didn't give me all of it and I had to go after him and get the rest."[61] As it was, the officers only had a partial still, mash and a tiny bit of liquor on the premises with which to indict the man. It is unknown how Klaver fared, as he was released on a $350 bond, and there was no further report of his either being arrested, jailed or sentenced.

Just the year before, a gallon of "white mule" went missing following a trial hearing. When a jug was brought into the sheriff's office, a seal was put on it to keep it in the condition in which it had arrived (i.e., in the jug). Sheriff Smith cracked the seal in the courtroom to confirm the presence of alcohol. However, when the jug was given back to the undersheriff the next day, it was discovered it contained nothing more than "ordinary aqua pura" from the city reservoir. The *Bozeman Courier* posed the question: "Was the stuff so strong that it just merely evaporated overnight under the influence of the warm Bear Creek atmosphere in the courthouse, or did it….But then one guess is just as good as another."[62]

In February 1925, Sheriff Smith made a public return on the department's recent successes in upholding Prohibition. According to Smith, his force had seized about thirteen gallons of moonshine, not a huge amount by any means. However, they had managed to find and destroy over nineteen partial to complete stills. In the case of more than one still, including one in the Sedan district, dynamite was used to blow up the operations, as they would have been too difficult and costly to bring to the county jail for evidence. The department also burned down several cabins in many of the canyons about Gallatin County, in hopes of deterring would-be moonshiners from setting up their operations there. Overall, it was noted that the copper from all these stills, weighing four hundred pounds, was sold for twenty-four dollars.[63]

Jack Johnson, a Scandinavian farmhand, was repeatedly booked for the possession, manufacture and selling of moonshine whiskey. Most cases like his can be looked back on with humor. The same man continually getting thrown in jail for moonshine brings up images of Otis from the *Andy Griffith Show*. However, Johnson's foray into moonshine turned deadly when, in 1923, on the day before Christmas, Stephen R. Maggard murdered his wife, Virginia Belle Maggard, before turning the gun on himself at their home on North Bozeman Avenue. The incident occurred just after noon. It appears that a conflict occurred when Mrs. Maggard came home from her job at a local laundry to prepare lunch for her husband. Stephen shot his wife twice in the neck—neither shot being fatal—before she ran for the door, trying to escape. Virginia must have fallen on the front porch, where her husband put a final bullet in her skull as she cried out for help. He then

Confiscated still items sitting outside the county jail during Prohibition in the 1920s. *Gallatin Historical Society/Gallatin History Museum.*

turned the gun on himself. Stephen would not succumb to his own self-inflicted would until several days later. It was believed that jealousy spurred on the attack; the couple had recently been separated, and Stephen was unhappy with a boarder that Virginia had taken on in their Bozeman home. They had argued about the situation on more than one occasion, which was attested to by their married daughter, Mrs. L.B. Cubbage. The couple had originally moved to Bozeman from Oklahoma two years prior, to be near their daughter. They also had two sons, Chester Maggard, who had had a few scrapes with the law, and Fred Maggard, who was fourteen years old at the time and in the house during the incident. Fred managed to escape during the affray.[64]

The connection to Johnson was indirect, but no less important for being so, in the events that took place. Many witnesses would attest to Stephen Maggard's lack of sobriety on numerous occasions, and it was believed that he had been drinking the night before the murder/suicide. This revelation tipped off Sheriff Jim Smith to send a force to the Maggard Ranch the night after the incident, where Johnson was found in the act of manufacturing moonshine whiskey. The "mash" was still hot when it was brought into the sheriff's office. Johnson was finally found guilty in March 1924, fined

$200 and sentenced to six months in jail, but he would be paroled on good behavior, having already served seventy-two days in jail awaiting his trial.[65]

It would remain a mystery whether Stephen Maggard had indeed been drunk the night before his rampage. One witness stated that she smelled liquor on his breath when he was awaiting his wife for his "noonday meal." The nurses attending to him that night, however, would state they smelled no odor of liquor. Regardless of what happened that night, Stephen's excessive drinking had led Mrs. Maggard to visit the sheriff's office just six weeks before her death, voicing concern over her safety, a fear that sadly became a grim reality.[66]

Johnson ended up back in jail on July 2, 1924, booked as "drunk." He was released three days later by Judge B.B. Law and seemed to stay out of trouble from then on.[67]

In 1926, the State of Montana voted to end Prohibition. While this did take effect, the Bozeman police force in no way became more lenient. According to a notice in the *Bozeman Courier* on November 12, 1926, Judge Wilson saw reason keep up a strict attentiveness to the liquor trade. Judge

Confiscated still in the collection of the Gallatin History Museum. *Image by Victoria Richard.*

Wilson stated: "Hitherto, in Bozeman, we have been arresting and punishing 'bootleggers' and 'moonshiners' as having violated a city ordinance which declares the liquor traffic to be a nuisance. We see no reason for changing or modifying that policy. Such traffic is still a nuisance that may and should be published under the quite large police powers granted to cities by the general laws under which cities are organized and operate." He then went on to list a few city codes, such as Subdivision 33, "to define and abate nuisances, and to impose fines upon persons guilty of creating" a nuisance, and Subdivision 25, "to prevent and punish intoxication, fights, riots, loud noises, disorderly conduct, obscenity and acts or conduct calculated to disturb the public peace." According to Judge Wilson: "There is nothing more productive of the foregoing offences than the liquor traffic. How shall we prevent such offences if no attempt is made to control and suppress the liquor traffic?"[68]

Chapter 4

SPEAKING ILL OF A COUNTRY

Sedition during World War I

I don't see why we should be fighting the kaiser and I don't see why people
should go crazy over patriotism. The kaiser and his government is better than
the United States and I would go over to Germany if I could.
—*Frank McVey, April 11, 1918*

*O*n April 11, 1918, Frank McVey, a laborer from Illinois, stepped into a Logan restaurant, about twenty-five miles from Bozeman. A complaint about sugar and a comment in support of the kaiser landed him in the local jail. He would spend the next three years of his life in the state penitentiary, convicted of sedition.

When the United States entered the Great War in 1917, it had already missed out on the first three years of battle because of the reluctance of both the government and U.S. citizens to participate in an overseas conflict. Since the beginning, however, private donors had been sending monetary donations and food to help those in need; in fact, America was the top philanthropic nation at the time. The U.S. government, upon entering the war, found it necessary to discourage antiwar sentiment in order to bolster public support of their involvement. The industry of public relations would be born during this decade of pro-war, patriotic propaganda. Never before had the nation's citizens had a calling quite like this to do their part, which included keeping an eye on your neighbor to be sure they, too, were lending a hand—or at least not condemning the effort.

SUGAR BOWLS UNDER BAN
IN ALL HOTELS AND CAFES

BOZEMAN, April 13.—"The sugar bowl must go from the tables of Montana's hotels and restaurants," said Food Administrator Atkinson last night. For some time the administration has been urging that sugar bowls be removed from tables and that sugar service be individual. Yesterday, however, the food administration changed its request to a formal order, which is being sent out to all hotels and restaurants in the state.

Article announcing the ban of the sugar bowl during World War I. *Gallatin Historical Society/ Gallatin History Museum.*

"Slacker" was a term commonly used during World War I to describe a person not participating in the war effort, particularly those avoiding military service. "Slacker raids" were made in an attempt to find evaders. While this term was not used across the pond in Britain, women in the Order of the White Feather addressed such perceived evasion of "duty." This group handed out white feathers, representing cowardice, in an attempt to force men and, in many cases, teenage boys into service through guilt. In America, during this time, "slackers" could be arrested and made to serve time or register for military duty if found guilty of evasion. In Bozeman, from the United States' first involvement in World War I to the armistice in 1918, nine men were arrested for this offense. Closely related was a "failure to register," another common offense. In total, eighteen men were held under investigations pertaining to wartime evasion. Five of these men were found either too young to serve or not fit for military service, one paid a ten-dollar fine and the remaining twelve either registered or were taken to a local military outpost, where, it is presumed, they committed to doing their duty. There were also thirteen cases of military desertion found in the Gallatin County Jail records.[69]

Among the "slackers" and deserters was another group of offenders, those who spoke or took action against either the government or the war efforts. The Espionage Act of 1917, followed closely by the Sedition Act, passed on May 16, 1918, resulted in citizen-promoted policing of neighbors. The government's attempt to keep the American people united in the war effort led to an overall panic, as many people feared their neighbors could be German sympathizers. This fear would escalate during WWII and the era

Frank McVey, sedition, 1918, Gallatin County Jail. *Gallatin Historical Society/Gallatin History Museum.*

of McCarthyism, during which, in many cases, the system led to an abuse of the law by those who sought to endanger those they disliked by claiming them unpatriotic. In Bozeman, twelve men were arrested for seditious behavior or remarks; four were found guilty. Two men would be sent to the state penitentiary, one being Frank McVey.

Frank was first arrested on April 11, 1918. The *Bozeman Weekly Courier* of April 17 printed a small article titled "Frank McVey Charged with Uttering Sedition," describing the scene that led to his arrest. It seems that McVey entered a restaurant and, seeing that there was not a sugar bowl on the table, "demanded that one be forthcoming." The proprietor told him that the Food Administration had abolished the sugar bowl in an effort to conserve supply, something that McVey found displeasing. According to the *Courier*, McVey "brought a sack of sugar from his pocket from which he put a liberal allowance in his coffee."[70] Proprietor C.S. Hopping and a patron, C.W. Clary, prevented his drinking the coffee. During the commotion, McVey allegedly remarked: "I don't see why we should be fighting the Kaiser and I don't see why people should go crazy over patriotism. The Kaiser and his government is better than the United States and I would go over to Germany if I could."[71] He was promptly arrested; the jail record stated a warrant was made out for the offense of sedition. However, it appears that on May 16, 1918, while McVey was in

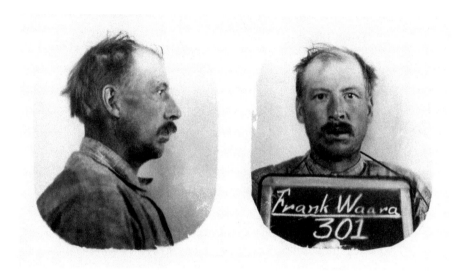

Frank Waara, sedition, 1918, Gallatin County Jail. *Gallatin Historical Society/Gallatin History Museum.*

custody, an additional warrant was completed on a complaint by Lee B. Anderson that McVey had unlawful possession of a firearm. It is unclear which warrant held him in jail, but he remained at the Gallatin County Jail until his court date. The trial was held June 3, and it took only ten minutes for the jury to bring back a verdict of guilty.[72] On the same day, Frank Waara was also tried for sedition; both men were found guilty and taken to the Montana State Prison on June 7. Their convictions made statewide news, as reported in the *Montana Record-Herald,* "Two Men Are Sentenced to Prison for Sedition."[73] Waara served eleven months of an eighteen-month-to-three-year sentence and McVey twenty-six months of a two-to-four-year sentence. By World War II, McVey was living in Pasco, Washington, unemployed at the age of sixty-three.[74]

Of the sixty arrests in Gallatin County related to World War I made between February 1917 and August 1919, Waara and McVey were the only two who served longer than a few days' jail sentence, illustrating the severity of being found guilty of sedition.

Montana's sedition law preceded that of the federal government. With the efforts of Montana's senators, Congress passed a sedition law three months after Montana, with only three words changed.[75] On May 3, 2006, the seventy-five men and three women sentenced for sedition in Montana were pardoned by Governor Brian Schweitzer.

Another law that came into prominence was the Alien Gun Law, which actually predated the United States' involvement in World War I by three years. This law made it illegal for noncitizens to carry a firearm. From 1914 to 1919, there were twenty-three violations of this law, and quite a few the offenders were brought in by the local game wardens. The fine for most was $27.50, about $720 in today's money, which most paid rather than serve the time. Those arrested for vagrancy in the valley in 1917 and 1918 found themselves put to work on Sheriff Del Gray's road gangs. With a lack of men in the area to do the work due to the war, those termed "loafers" and "slackers" were made into a substitute work force. In 1918, they were primarily working on road repair and maintenance. Refusal to work would be punished with a diet of bread and water.[76]

Chapter 5

WHAT IS IN A NAME?

Forgery and Embezzlement

Finest fruit land in the country.
—*A fraudulent 1912 Yellowstone National Park Land Company advertisement*
for land in the region of Bozeman, Montana,
a town situated at seven thousand feet

In 1878, an interesting case of fraudulent banking took hold of the Gallatin Valley, when the Bank of Bozeman closed its doors. The articles about the case are confusing, but it seems that George W. Fox, a banker, had written an entry for $6,000 as a draft to an eastern bank, which had been determined fraudulent, quite possibly as a coverup for a deposit that Fox made and removed for personal use. It seems that Fox had embezzled the money, entrusted to the bank by local account holders, for personal use. A grand jury pronounced seven indictments against Fox, fixing his bond at $14,000, which, since he was unable to pay it, sent him to the county jail at Lewis and Clark County to await his trial date. According to a letter from Helena to the *Bozeman Avant Courier* from January 1879, it was believed that Fox was to make his new residence at the Deer Lodge Penitentiary at a coming date. Information from a Mr. Willson, receiver of the Bozeman Bank, seemed to be the final straw in the case against Fox. Throughout the trial, Fox seemed to take the whole matter rather easily and did not seem concerned. Granville Stuart, Montana pioneer and receiver of the People's National Bank in Helena (associated with the Bank of Bozeman and Fox), was called as a witness. When arguments concluded, it seems the jury was stuck in disagreement for many days. They spent a whole night together deliberating and were taken on a walk about town by the sheriff before being locked back up to deliberate some more. After seventy-two hours, they were still in disagreement and were discharged.[77]

In May 1879, Fox was still being held at the jail awaiting a new trial. According to the *Bozeman Avant Courier*, Fox, "inmate of the iron bound brick mansion on Court Square, grimly chuckles that he will make some startling revelations when his trial comes off."[78] By August, Fox, was exhibiting a much different look and manner. It was noted that he looked "utterly broken down physically and mentally....He is pale and emaciated, and if appearances may be relied on, not long for this world." For a time, friends had brought the man meals, but an attempted jail escape that summer curtailed that privilege. It was said that Fox would cry and state that if he went to the pen, leading citizens in Helena were going to go with him.[79]

By December 1879, the court was still occupied with the Fox case, and it looked like it would be March before a new trial could be granted. By this time, there had been two mistrials. Those bank account holders in Bozeman and Helena who were victimized by the man anxiously awaited punishment for his actions. On August 19, 1880, it was announced that Fox had been discharged. By March 1881, the *River Press* out of Fort Benton noted that a George W. Fox had sailed from San Francisco for the Holy Land and "if it is the Fox against whom so many charges were docketed in the Montana courts, he is certainly a 'sly one.'"[80] While the suits against him would remain, the man seems to have gotten away from his predicament with only the eighteen months he spent in jail awaiting his trials.

On June 18, 1912, the citizens of Bozeman awoke to the headline "County Fund Shortage Sends Treasurer C. Corbly to Jail." It seems the popular treasurer was accused of embezzling from $18,000 to $20,000 when a shortage of that amount was discovered by deputy examiners Williams and Hoss. According to Corbly, the shortage had existed for a number of years, and he had endeavored to cover it up at each examination by depositing checks with banks other than where the checks were drawn until the examiner left, then not charging the checks. It had been his plan to make up the deficit by 1913. Corbly had been in the service of the county for fourteen years and county treasurer since 1909, easily winning reelection due to his popularity in the county.[81]

Rumors rapidly spread as to Corbly's personal financial stability. While many related that Corbly neither smoked nor drank and did not lead an expensive social life nor seem in any way in need of funds, others questioned

The National Bank of Gallatin Valley (First West Insurance), located on the northwest corner of the intersection of Tracy Avenue and Main Street in Bozeman, circa 1940s. *Gallatin Historical Society/Gallatin History Museum.*

Montana Bank of Bozeman in 1976. *Gallatin Historical Society/Gallatin History Museum.*

whether the income on which Corbly lived had been enough to sustain his family. The most curious part of Corbly's statements regarding the case against him was his plan to cover up the deficit permanently with his own personal money. It was then widely believed that officials had just been doing their duty in arresting Corbly, and the matter would soon be cleared up and Corbly exonerated.[82]

By the following month, however, things had begun to look grim for Corbly, as additional shortages had been discovered, bringing the total deficit to $26,000. When Corbly was first arrested, his bond was set at $20,000, the amount of deficit at the time, then lowered to $5,000, as it seemed the accused was going to be able to remedy the situation. When the extra deficit was discovered, his bond was raised to $25,000, meaning Corbly would have to stay in the Gallatin County Jail until his trial date.[83] Another month would pass before Corbly would answer to the charges against him. In the end, he chose a plea of not guilty. At his initial hearing, it was said that Corbly was one of the "most disinterested persons in the court room."[84] In spite of the charges against him, Corbly still insisted that he could make up the deficit. It seems he had recently copyrighted a delinquent tax record book that he believed was of great value, and he believed that from the sales of this book, he could make up the shortage. A demurrer was entered, stating that the amounts had not been clarified, so Corbly could speak to each one. This and his plea for a lessened bond, so he could make up the funds, were both initially denied, and it was then Corbly made his plea of not guilty, sealing his fate. The bond was eventually reduced to $15,000, and a sufficient amount was raised to release the man from the confines of the county jail after over two months of confinement. The list of bondsmen included farmers, butchers, grain dealers, postmasters, teamsters and a housewife.[85] A business ad soon appeared in *Republican-Courier* advertising a sales and purchase agent with "Special Attention to Tax Matters and Collections." The name of the agent? Clyde Corbly.

In October, Corbly had asked for a change of venue, believing his trial would not be impartial if held in Gallatin County; the motion was denied. At the start of the new year, 1913, Clyde was again sitting in jail awaiting his trial, which was postponed due to the judge being absent. Corbly had been rearrested when a new set of deficits had been discovered, amounting to $400. A suit was officially filed against the United States Fidelity and Guaranty Company, which bonded Corbly as the county treasurer for a grand total of $25,474.49. It would not be until March 1913, almost a year after his initial arrest, that Clyde Corbly would face his trial.[86]

Cribbage board carved into the table that was used for prisoner's leisure activities. *Author's image.*

March 18, 1913, marked the start of the trial, a day having been used already in determining the jury. Witnesses were placed on the stand who testified that Corbly knew a deficit existed and that he had tried, through innuendo, to place the blame on his predecessor, Weaver, and Weaver's

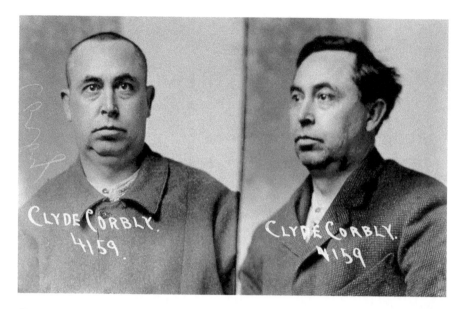

Clyde Corbly, feloniously appropriating public moneys to his use, 1913, prison, Deer Lodge, Montana. *Montana Historical Society.*

children. The defense made efforts to show Corbly's intent to use his own funds to repair a deficit that had not been his; however, this attempt was to no avail.[87] On March 26, 1913, it was announced that, after six hours of deliberation, the jury had brought back a verdict of guilty. It was noted that the jury asked for leniency in the punishment, to which Judge J.B. Poindexter stated in his sentencing of Corbly that he regretted the maximum punishment had been set so low, as he would have given the full ten years if he could. It was noted that over one hundred people had been unable to get into the packed courtroom to hear the verdict. Corbly's wife was absent the last two days of the trial, and their children were never brought into the courtroom. In reply to the defense's plea, on behalf of the family of Clyde Corbly, for leniency, prosecuting attorney Patten stated, "Almost always the defendant asks the jury to remember those whom he has forgotten." On Tuesday, March 25, 1913, Corbly was taken to the Deer Lodge State Prison, where he was sentenced to serve five to eight and a half years.[88]

Another case of embezzlement would occur in 1913, that of Ben Winters Shirk, former bookkeeper for Thomas B. Quaw's grocery store. Young Shirk had "tapped the till" for $155.73, which he spent in showing his friends a good time with dancing, theater and dinner parties. Shirk was sentenced to

PINKERTON'S NATIONAL DETECTIVE AGENCY.

FOUNDED BY ALLAN PINKERTON 1850.

ROB'T A. PINKERTON, New York. } Principals.
WM. A. PINKERTON, Chicago.

GEO. D. BANGS, GENERAL MANAGER, New York.
ALLAN PINKERTON, ASS'T GEN'L M'G'R, New York.

JOHN CORNISH, MANAGER, Eastern Division, New York.
EDW. S. GAYLOR, MANAGER, Middle Division, Chicago.

JAS. McPARLAND, MANAGER, Western Division, Denver.
J. C. FRASER, MANAGER, Pacific Division, San Francisco.

—OFFICES.—

NEW YORK	57 Broadway.	CHICAGO	201 Fifth Avenue.	DENVER	Opera House Block
BOSTON	30 Court Street.	CLEVELAND	Garfield Building.	OMAHA	New York Life Building
MONTREAL	Merchants Bank Building.	CINCINNATI	Mercantile Library Building.	SPOKANE	Rookery Building.
BUFFALO	Fidelity Building.	ST. PAUL	Manhattan Building.	SEATTLE	Alaska Building.
PHILADELPHIA	441 Chestnut Street.	ST. LOUIS	Walnwright Building.	PORTLAND, ORE.	Marquam Block.
BALTIMORE	Continental Building.	KANSAS CITY	622 Main Street.	LOS ANGELES	Wilcox Building.
PITTSBURGH	Machesney Building.			SAN FRANCISCO	927 Eddy Street.

REPRESENTING
THE AMERICAN BANKERS' ASSOCIATION.

SPOKANE,
ROOKERY BUILDING,
G. J. HASSON, SUP'T.

$100⁰⁰ REWARD

The American Bankers' Association offer a Reward of One Hundred Dollars for the arrest, detention and surrender to proper authorities of A. O., alias Albert West, alias Fred Laranger, who, on April 4th, 1907, swindled the First National Bank of Great Falls, Montana, by means of a bogus check, purporting to have been signed by E. W. Ellis of Millegan, Montana, by whom he was employed as a sheepherder from November, 1906 to April, 1907.

DESCRIPTION

AGE . . . . 35 to 40 years
HEIGHT . . . 5 feet 10 or 11 inches
WEIGHT . . . . about 165 pounds
BUILD . . . . Medium
EYES . . . . Blue
COMPLEXION . . . . . Light
HAIR . . . Medium dark or brown
BEARD : Brown, probably smooth shaven. Short, stubby beard when last seen.

FAC-SIMILE OF HANDWRITING

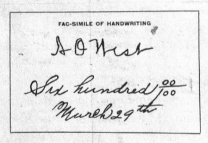

REMARKS : Large nose, receding chin. Wears glasses. Speaks with Southern accent, slight impediment in speech. Hard of hearing. Teeth poor and gold filled. Apparently well educated. Good writer.

The above forger claims to be a native of Alabama, and is said to have previously worked as a sheepherder in the vicinity of White Sulphur Springs, Montana, and also in a sugar factory at Billings, Montana. He has also traveled in or been employed in North Dakota.

If located, arrest and notify the undersigned by wire to their nearest office, listed above.

15 A.M.

PINKERTON'S NATIONAL DETECTIVE AGENCY

306 ROOKERY BUILDING
SPOKANE, WASHINGTON

OR G. J. HASSON
RESIDENT SUPT.
SPOKANE, WASH., MAY 29, 1907

TELEPHONE MAIN 234
NIGHT PHONE MAIN 6647

Wanted poster for a forger from the Pinkerton National Detective Agency, in a collection of "wanted" memorabilia sent to and from the Gallatin County Jail. *Gallatin Historical Society/Gallatin History Museum.*

one year at Deer Lodge State Prison. At the date of his sentencing, Shirk was just eighteen years old.[89]

Cases of the more corporate nature included many a fake company drummed up to sell land to unsuspecting easterners who had not yet visited the Gallatin Valley. One such company was exposed by *Republican-Courier* in 1910, but the case did not come to a conclusion until an official investigation was completed and an arrest made in March 1912. It seems H.A. Mason, secretary and treasurer, and John A. Hanley, director, of the Yellowstone National Land Company based out of Chicago, had been arrested and charged with the use of mail to defraud. Over five thousand acres of Gallatin and Madison County land had been advertised by the pair as some of the "finest fruit land in the country." Those living in the valley at the time would have immediately seen the issue with advertising land at seven thousand feet as fine fruit-growing country. One such man, W.R. Finlay, had fallen for the trick and bought land that he discovered, upon arrival, was only good for raising hay. The commissioner of the State Bureau of Agriculture, J.H. Hall, was alerted to the situation when a resident of Iowa sent in an inquiry on the "orchard tracts" advertised. According to Hall, the scheme was the "rottenest concern" he had ever encountered.[90]

Forgery was an often-cited crime in the annals of the jail registry books. From 1893 to 1935, there were 155 arrests, with nearly seventy of the perpetrators sent to the state penitentiary in Deer Lodge. The youngest offender was fifteen years old. Those who were underage were taken to the reform school in Great Falls. One particularly frightening case was that of a physician, Dr. E.H. Thomas, who fraudulently conducted medical activities while not a licensed physician and was sent to Deer Lodge for four years on a forgery charge.

In 1913, Kemp Parsons, seventeen years old, made the rounds of Bozeman, Billings and Nebraska. Kemp became familiar in each town with the names of the local residents and, with the "artistic work" of his pen, could forge their names with ease.[91] He was taken into custody on July 11, 1913, then moved to the Deaconess Hospital three weeks later, where he died on August 20, 1913. Interestingly, one story of his short life states that Kemp had been fighting a fire in the Tobacco Root Mountains and was overcome with smoke. He was brought back to the hospital, where died. Unfortunately, the jail records show something quite different: he had clearly been incarcerated in the weeks before his death, not fighting a fire. His death certificate states he died from tubercular meningitis; how he contracted it is unknown.

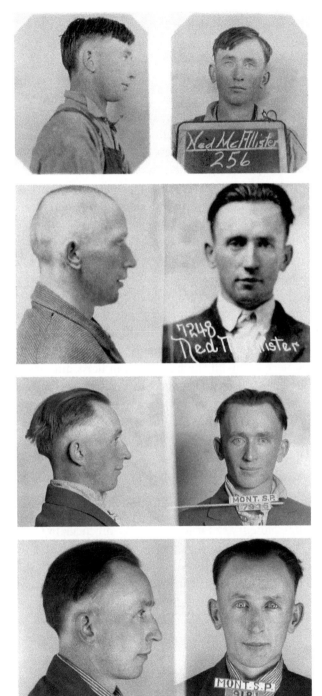

Ned McAllister, forgery, 1917, 1921, 1924 and 1929. First photo taken at the Gallatin County Jail. *Gallatin Historical Society/ Gallatin History Museum.* Three subsequent photos taken at the prison in Deer Lodge, Montana. *Montana Historical Society.*

Forgers, like liquor law violators, tended to be repeat offenders. One such case was Ned McAllister, initially arrested on November 16, 1917, for forging a check in Bozeman and sentenced to one to six years. He would be arrested again and sent to the pen on December 24, 1921, for a sentence of three to six years. He had only been out of prison for five months. Ned would be paroled on June 15, 1924, but back in prison in Belgrade, Montana, on December 22 on another forgery charge. He would again be paroled on January 20, 1929, spending less than four months out before being arrested again on a charge of forgery committed in Bozeman. This time, his sentence was for thirty months. He seems to have stayed in the area, passing away on April 17, 1958, at the Montana State Tuberculosis Sanitorium.[92]

On December 13, 1927, Mildred Tandy was arrested on a forgery charge, having put Mrs. M.A. Griffin's name on a check for fifteen dollars, which she cashed at the Bozeman pharmacy. While she was in jail, another forgery came to light: a forged check in the name of Stuart McMillan, which she had used at the Marshall furniture store. Mildred pleaded guilty and received a sentence of four to eight years at the penitentiary. The night of her arrest, she attempted to take her own life in her prison cell by severing the blood vessels in her wrist with a piece of metal she had found in her vanity case. Two days later, on December 15, the man who had been posing as her husband, Joe Tandy, was arrested on an adultery charge. It seems Mildred's real name was Mildred McMillan; Stuart McMillan was her real husband. She was released into the custody of her father, to live with him for four years on parole. Life seems to have taken a turn for the better, however, when, on January 21, 1928, Mildred visited Bozeman with her new husband, Joe Tandy, stating that "everything now was all right."[93]

A similar penalty was given to R.M. Sutherland, who received a sentence of four to eight years in the penitentiary for forging a $47.50 check in G.D. McCarty's name at the Men's Store. More checks of a similar nature had been found on his person while he was at the jail.[94]

In the summer of 1930, the husband-and-wife team Henry and Catherine Hinkley forged twenty-dollar checks at three different stores after banking hours, all in the name of L.E. Henderson. The couple was caught in Pocatello, Idaho, due to the quick work of Sheriff O.L. DeVore. Catherine received a sentence of one year and her husband one of twenty months. Henry was discharged on October 27, 1931, but sent back to the penitentiary on January 20, 1939, on another forgery charge, this time in Miles City. His marital status at this point was "separated." He was to serve one year, which

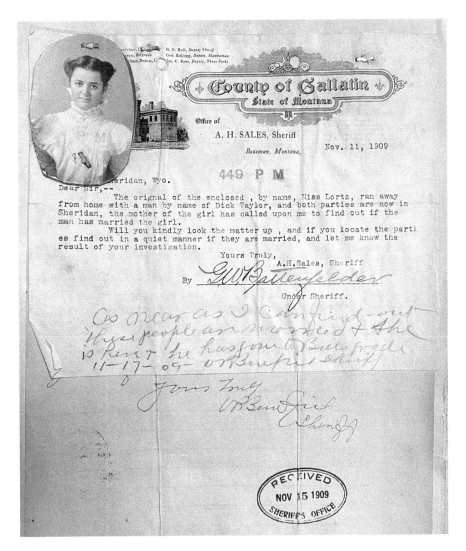

Letter to Sheridan, Wyoming, inquiring into the marital status of Miss Lortz, who had run away from the Bozeman area with a Dick Taylor. 1909. *Gallatin Historical Society/Gallatin History Museum.*

he did; however, on January 4, 1943, he was again back in Deer Lodge for a check forgery committed in Dillon, Montana. This time, his sentence was set at four years, and his marital status was "divorced." His prison record had twenty-seven arrests spanning from 1926 to 1943. It is unknown if Catherine followed a similar or different life path; one can assume that, after her stint in prison and distancing herself from her husband, she may have gone on

Above: Museum exhibit that allows visitors to take their mug shot using the same door and measuring bar that was used in the jail. *Author's image.*

Opposite: Henry Hinkley, forgery, booked 1930, 1939 and 1943, prison, Deer Lodge, Montana. *Montana Historical Society.*

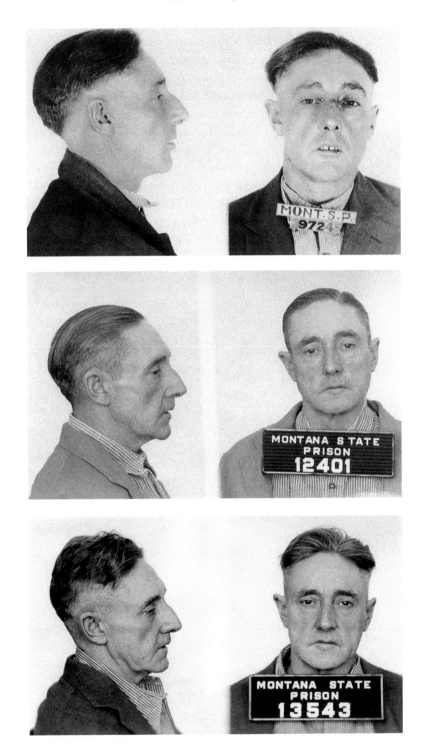

the straight. Interestingly, Henry's first prison record lists his wife's address as Box 7, Deer Lodge, Montana. One wonders if they saw each other again after her release.[95]

A humorous story of a forger took place in 1944, when repeat check "artist" E. Russell Schroeder received a repeat jail sentence. It seems that Schroeder had spent thirty days as a "star boarder" at the jail when a local resident paid his fifty-dollar fine on a loan after hearing his hard luck story. Schroeder got an eight-dollar-a-day job in a hayfield, which lasted one half day before he passed another check and departed from the area. Unfortunately for Schroeder, local Gallatin officers were able to trail him to a bar in Wisdom, where he was found asleep on a pool table, and promptly hauled him back to Bozeman, where he was fined seventy-five dollars and "given another extended invitation to the county jail for 60 days."[96]

she was fined $25. Following this was a case against Josephine Merrill and Oscar Merrill, who were found guilty of "keeping and maintaining a house of ill fame" at that same address. Each was fined $50 for this offense and an additional $100 each for possessing moonshine whiskey.[101] In October 1927, another raid was conducted at 221 East Mendenhall, where Mr. and Mrs. Carl Pugh and Mr. and Mrs. Arthur Mayfield were arrested for maintaining a "disorderly house." Mrs. Pugh was fined $75 and the Mayfields $50 each. Earlier that year, in September, Tom Brooks and Freda Fields had been arrested on the same charge and each fined $25.

On April 12, 1912, Marshall Gore was arrested for possessing and passing indecent letters and pictures about the town. He was arrested at 2:10 in the morning by Undersheriff Battenfelder and Patrolman Smullen at his home, while he was in the act of drawing an indecent picture. It seems Gore confessed to creating over 250 different obscene letters and drawings, which he often placed in areas where unsuspecting women would pick them up, not knowing what they were until they opened them. The officers were able to finally catch the man at work, with the help of a decoy note. Gore had left a note on a clothesline of the Strong Hotel, which he had addressed to a girl who worked there. The officers found it and placed a fake note in the envelope in place of what Gore hoped would be the girl's response, then waited for Gore to retrieve the note. When he did, about midnight, the officers quietly followed the man home and watched through a window, where they observed him creating one of his obscene drawings. The officers were able to sneak through the house, passing through rooms where Gore's family slept before coming to stand quietly next to the man in his kitchen. They went unnoticed until one of the officers nudged the man sitting at his table, to his horror. It was said that Gore lost all speech until he made it to the jail.[102]

The *Republican-Courier* noted that the drawings showed artistic ability, while the lettering seemed like that of a trained draftsman. Many of the drawings had been neatly done on the pages of a ledger book, then carefully wrapped up and placed on the porches of houses where young girls lived. The paper stated that "although the crime is a heinous one, it is feared that nothing more than a misdemeanor can be charged." The capture of Gore was much applauded by the author of the article as a major feather in the cap of the local police force.[103] Unfortunately, the columns pertaining to Gore's release and sentencing were left empty in the jail records, so it is unknown what he paid for his crime of terrorizing the city for months.

Chapter 7

THIS IS A HOLDUP

Bank Robberies

As the first dry clods rattled on the gray caskets containing the bodies
of the dead bandits, the clock hands pointed to the same hour...they had
indicated just a week before, when the two men, with guns drawn,
entered the Security Bank and Trust
—*The* Bozeman Daily Chronicle, *July 30, 1932*

n December 5, 1923, the front page of the *Bozeman Courier*
described a "sensational raid" at Havre, where eight out of twelve
bank robbers were apprehended. The arrests were on the heels
of their twenty-sixth holdup at the State Bank in Salesville, just thirteen
miles west of Bozeman. Gallatin County sheriff Jim Smith had worked
with detectives and officers from Madison and Hill Counties on the trail
of this gang of "professional cracksmen." Six men and two women were
rounded up in Havre, after which Sheriff Smith departed for Salt Lake
City to bring back the other four, Adolph Melcher, George Dyer, Tom
Martin and Frank Warren, who were to be extradited to Montana for the
prosecution.[104]

Rae Davis, the wife of the man who would "pour the soup" (nitroglycerine
used to destroy locks), was taken by Smith to Helena for examination and
detention. According to the jail ledger, H.E. Loranger (former sheriff of
Hill County), Frank Warren, Adolph Mechler, Thomas Martin, George
Dyer and Ed Marshall were all booked at the Gallatin County Jail for

WICKED BOZEMAN

26 BANK ROBBERIES IN
STATE IN THREE YEARS

The following robberies and attempted robberies of banks have
taken place in Montana in the past
three years:

1921

April 11—Farmers State bank of
Coburg.
May 18—Willow Creek State bank.
Aug. 8—Sumatra State bank.
Aug. 29—First National bank of
Plains.
Sept. 18—Homestead State bank.
Sept. 21—First National bank of
Denton.

1922

April 29—State bank of Madoc.
June 10—Dayton State bank.
June 13—First National bank of
Roy.
June 27—Corvallis State bank.
July 14—Farmers and Merchants
bank, Dixon.
July 27—First State bank of Clyde
Park.
Aug. 31—Farmers State bank of
Glentana.
Oct. 17—First National bank of
Fairfield.
Nov. 16—The Sheridan State bank.

1923

April 17—First National bank of
Valier.
May 10—Farmers State bank of
Gildford.
**May 21—First State bank of Wil-
liams.**
May 23—Camas State bank of Hot
Springs.
June 11—Farmers and Merchants
State bank of Plains.
Aug. 14—Blair & Co., State bank
of Helmville.
Sept. 5—Citizens State bank of
Clyde Park.
Sept. 17—Southern Montana State
bank of Ennis.
Oct. 19—Granite County bank of
Hall.
Nov. 6—First National bank of
Fairfield.
Nov. 10—Salesville State bank. .

List of bank robberies conducted by
the gang. *Bozeman Courier*, December
5, 1923. *Gallatin Historical Society/
Gallatin History Museum.*

participation in the Salesville robbery. Loranger was released on a $500 bail, no trial; Warren was released to Madison County, where he was sentenced to the penitentiary; Mechler was released to the sheriff of Virginia City; Martin was sentenced to six and a half to fifteen years in the pen; Dyer got seven and a half to fifteen years in the pen; and Marshall was released by order of Judge B.B. Law. It is unknown where the rest of the gang were detained. While at the county jail, one of the men refused butter, stating, "It's rotten. It came from Salesville."[105]

It was clear that Gallatin County was very proud of its participation in the arrests of this criminal gang. It was said that when a Hill County officer asked Sheriff Smith if "all the men in Gallatin County were as big and husky as he," he replied, "I should say they are. Why, I'm a good deal smaller than the average run of men in my bailiwick."[106] The pride grew the next week, when Sheriff Smith was credited by the Salt Lake Police and newspapers as the discoverer of two stolen bonds, which would be vital evidence in the case against the gang. Smith had found the bonds buried in a mason jar in the backyard of a shack in Salt Lake. Along with the bonds were found mason jars with tools of the bank robber's trade, including dynamite caps and fuses. Also on the premises were found expensive tools for cracking safes, nitroglycerine, torches and chisels, which were all used by experienced "yeggmen." It was believed that Adolph Mechler—one of the men brought from Salt Lake, who stated he was a lace peddler—was the man who found the "marks," banks that seemed easy to rob, while on his travels.[107]

It seems the gang had been the scheme of a man named Reed, who had made successful robberies in Canada, one amounting to $100,000. "Bad Eye" George Dyer, who had recently been paroled from the Montana State Penitentiary, was believed to have been the master yeggman, having been convicted as such prior. By December 26, three more men had been caught, including Reed, who was taken to Great Falls.[108]

The case against the gang would continue to develop over the next month, with news coming in weekly on trial dates and interesting stories appearing in the press about those involved. On February 20, 1924, it was announced that the sheriffs who had worked with the Burns detective agency—a national agency founded by W.J. Burns, former secret service official in the Treasury Department—on the case had criticisms of the agency and of Walter Gordon, who represented the agency specifically. Gordon was apparently trying to undermine the efforts of law enforcement and was attempting to make his own deals with the prisoners to retrieve the bonds. The Burns detective agency, and ones like it, often made their money off rewards offered by retrieving bonds. It seems that Sheriff Smith had retrieved over $100,000 worth of the stolen bonds, more than any other sheriff in any other county, with no intention of accepting the rewards associated with their return. In one instance, $3,000 worth of bonds belonging to a Great Falls woman could have netted him a $500 reward, but Smith was noted as saying the woman needed every dime she had. This difference was causing issues in getting the prisoners to cooperate. According to the *Courier*, however, Jim Smith had been able to strike a deal with Marshall to find the stolen bonds in return for a lighter sentence.[109]

The trial that was supposed to be almost as sensational as that of Seth Danner, charged with murder the previous year, was averted completely in March 1924. Sheriff Smith was given credit for saving the county over $2,500 by gaining the confidence of Ed "Daddy" Marshall, a principal witness in the case against the Salesville bank robbers. As a result, they all pleaded guilty, throwing themselves at the mercy of the court. It was only through the sale of the bonds to Marshall that the other men were implicated in the case. His was the only evidence against them.

The way in which Sheriff Smith was able to gain his confidence was a fascinating twist of fate. It seems that a letter had been mailed to Dyer, then at the county jail, from Salt Lake, which contained some simple notes in pencil and a quantity of strychnine between two sheets of paper. Smith intercepted the letter and realized it was either an attempt by someone outside to get poison into the hands of Dyer—who could then do away with Marshall

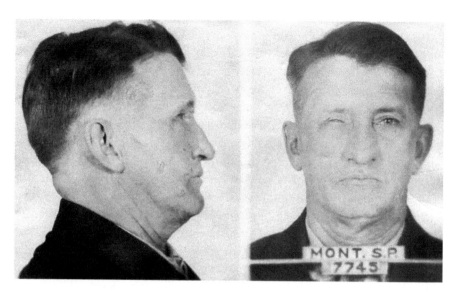

George Dyer, burglary first degree, 1924, prison, Deer Lodge, Montana. *Montana Historical Society.*

before he could testify, by inserting the poison into Marshall's "regular tray of jail fare"—or as an attempt to simply scare Marshall into silence. The act did not work, and instead, Marshall saw Smith as his saving grace, having protected him from possible death. In the end, both Dyer and Martin were sentenced to the pen due to Marshall's cooperation.[110]

This would not be the only bank robbery case to become a sensation in the area. A decade later, in the summer of 1932, two men would hold up the Security Bank and Trust Company at gunpoint for about $4,000. According to the *Bozeman Courier*, this was the first bank robbery to occur in Bozeman. The two men held cashiers Berthot, Street and Gossack, along with bookkeeper Mrs. Browning, at gunpoint with a six-shooter and a sawed-off shotgun while they took the money and pushed the group into a vault. Within fifteen minutes of their departure in a car, the alarm had been given, and every county sheriff within two hundred miles was on the alert.[111]

The two men, traveling in a green Ford coupe, were soon spotted getting gas at Karst Kamp. From there, Paul Bohart, employed at the camp, was asked to follow them on his motorcycle. Bohart soon caught up to them and opened fire on their car with a rifle he had borrowed from the Smith ranch. The men stopped the car to return fire, and soon all three were out in the woods, taking cover under heavy fire on both sides. Bohart made his escape and called for help.

For two days, a search was conducted for the men, to no avail—until word came that the two bandits had been seen at the cabin of Bud Henke. Henke, his wife, Hannah, and two other married couples, Buzzy and Oscar Keyes and Lyle and Daisy Richards, had gone up to the cabin that weekend for a fun getaway. In fact, on their way up, they had stopped at Karst for supplies; there, they met with a ranger, whom they invited to play pinochle with them that night. When they heard footsteps on the wood of the cabin's front porch and a knock came, those inside were expecting to see the ranger; instead, the barrel of a gun came through the door. The men demanded food, which they were given, but wanting to be prepared, they gave Henke ten dollars, telling him to go to the Wilson's 320 Ranch for groceries. Stories differ as to how many of those at the cabin went with Henke. When Henke arrived at the ranch, he found members of the posse, whom he told about the bandits, begging no one to come near the cabin, fearing that those inside would be killed. In an interview, when asked what the party at the cabin was thinking, Henke's daughter Helen Backlin stated, "They were scared of course….Dad had to drive to Karst and they all had to keep from causing tempers to flare, they all had to keep calm to survive."[112] According to a remembrance printed in the *Bozeman Daily Chronicle* on September 19, 1994, one of the people held at the cabin stated that the younger man played all the dance music records he could find on the phonograph, asking one of the women to dance with him.[113] The members of the Henke party would all look back over the years and

Sawed-off shotgun from a collection donated by the Law and Justice Center. *Gallatin Historical Society/Gallatin History Museum.*

think how foolish it may have been for them to make their escape to their cars after they were left alone by the bandits. The path was wide open, and a shot could have been fired from anywhere, but no shot came, and they escaped unscathed.

The posse was lying in wait outside the cabin when one of the men appeared. Upon his identification by Paul Bohart, a shot was taken at the man, hitting him in the left side of the chest. The man fell, instantly dead. When searched later, he was found to have $1,775 on his person, which was taken back to Bozeman immediately, with the request for an ambulance to bring back the dead man. (Only about $100 would remain unrecovered, in the end.) The posse then began a cautious search around the cabin. As Sheriff DeVore was conducting a slow search near a large rock, the remaining bandit appeared from behind some sagebrush and took three quick shots, all of which hit DeVore. He then shot at two other members of the posse, Allen Sales and Lester Pierstorff, who both dodged the bullets by diving for the ground. Each fired back, both hitting their mark, and the bandit quickly fell, dead. DeVore was taken back to Karst, where he received initial medical attention before spending three weeks in the Deaconess hospital. A bullet to his neck left him paralyzed in his left arm for a while, having just missed the jugular vein by a quarter of an inch.[114]

The 320 Ranch in Gallatin Canyon, 1935. *Gallatin Historical Society/Gallatin History Museum.*

Left: Sheriff O.L. DeVore, Gallatin County sheriff from 1929 to 1933. *Gallatin Historical Society/Gallatin History Museum.*

Right: Sheriff O.L. DeVore standing where one of the bandits shot at him. *From a 1937 issue of* Official Detective Stories Magazine.

Following this unfortunate outcome, the two men were brought to the Dokken Funeral Home, where curious men, women and children streamed through in an endless line that Monday, well into the night, to view the dead men. It was said that cars lined the streets next to the county jail awaiting the posse's return, while hundreds headed for the hospital to see DeVore arrive. A Pinkerton detective was present to photograph the men and take their fingerprints for identification.[115] The death certificates for the men read "Heavy John Doe" and "Shorty John Doe," with justifiable homicide as the cause of death from gunshots wounds. Their occupation: "bank robber.[116]

As dramatized in the *Bozeman Daily Chronicle* of July 30, 1932:

> *As the first dry clods rattled on the gray caskets containing the bodies of the dead bandits, the clock hands pointed to the same hour…they had indicated just a week before, when the two men, with guns drawn, entered the Security Bank and Trust….Only the nicknames "Heavy" and "Shorty" distinguish*

the metal markers placed at the head of the double grave into which the men's bodies were lowered....About 50 people, mostly women attended the short burial service....Mrs. Spangler sang.

The men were interred at Sunset Hills Cemetery. Homegrown flowers and wreaths surrounded the two caskets, all anonymously given by residents of the town.

The identities of the men would remain confused for quite some time. Even at the announcement of their burials, the two men were known only as "heavy" and "shorty." At first, the names Holt and Downey were given, then Charles Larrison and Curtis Bardell. Eventually, Paul Rushton and Andrew Hunter seem to be the two that were settled upon. Rushton had been an ex-con, charged with robbery and paroled from the Idaho penitentiary, who sometimes went by the name Paul Holt. According to records from Idaho, Rushton's mother wrote to the governor of Idaho and the penitentiary warden, requesting that they turn away any inquiries they received about her son and pretend he hadn't been there. It seems her husband was running for sheriff and wanted to avoid a scandal. This was just prior to her son's death following the bank robbery.[117] The young man with him, Hunter, had no previous criminal record and seems to have fallen under the wing of the wrong man, a fatal mistake. In later years, Andrew Hunter would be positively identified and his body sent to his mother in Missouri.

Within a week, Seth and Paul Bohart and Ed Lyons had applied for the $2,000 reward with the Montana Bankers Association for the capture of the first bandit.[118] A disagreement over who would receive the $2,000 for the second bandit ensued. In the end, the event proved costly to Seth Bohart, who lost the race for county attorney due to the conflicting stories of young Andrew Hunter's death.

A recounting of the event would appear in the February 1937 issue of *Official Detective Stories*, in which Seth Bohart was interviewed by M.M. Atwater. In 1937, the whole affray was dramatized on a New York City radio show hosted by Floyd Gibbons, based on Buzzy Keyes's account. Keyes was invited to New York, where she received a tour of Radio City Music Hall. Her children still have a metal record with a recording of the radio show, as well as letters she wrote to their father while in New York. They vividly remember listening to the recording over and over again in their childhood. According to Keyes, the experience of being held hostage had not changed her life for better or worse, but it proved to bring much

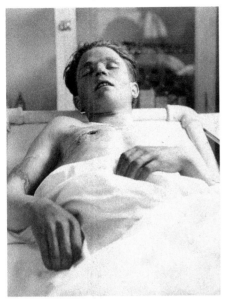 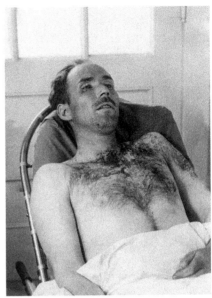

Left: Andrew Hunter, July 22, 1932. *Gallatin Historical Society/Gallatin History Museum.*

Right: Paul Rushton, July 22, 1932. *Gallatin Historical Society/Gallatin History Museum.*

entertainment over the years for all of those involved as well as magazine readers and radio audiences across the country.[119]

In speaking with the children of those who were involved in the incident at the cabin, one finds that, while slight details differed in their remembrances, a few things were in complete unison. The newspaper accounts left out an important part of the story. The young bandit who was killed first was murdered, without a chance of surrender. Those who were present state that the young man had his hands up in surrender when he was killed. Kenneth Keyes, son of Buzzy and Oscar Keyes, noted that was the way the times were. You were guilty until proven innocent; vigilante justice was still in the blood of the land. In a neat coincidence, Karen Keyes Street, daughter of Buzzy and Oscar, later married David Street, the son of a teller who was at the bank the day of the robbery. According to Karen, David remembered his dad, Joseph Dewey Street, saying that the younger bandit with the sawed-off shotgun was shaking so badly from nerves that Dewey was worried the gun would go off. That was the second thing all the remembrances included: the nervous state of young Andrew Hunter. The third thing they all mentioned was how scared those at the cabin had been. What was supposed to be a fun excursion into the mountains had quickly turned into a life-or-death situation. Interestingly, the effects of that trauma did not seem to alter their lives much. Despite all the fear and anxiety, it seems the experience simply became an exciting story to reiterate in the years to come: the story of the first bank robbery in Bozeman, Montana.

Chapter 8

A MOST EXPENSIVE PHEASANT

Game Law Violations and Other Oddities

"It was a great shot that brought it down—a shot to be proud of."
The deputy responded "Possibly so, but I don't think you'll be so proud of it
when I tell you it will prove the costliest bird you ever killed"
to which the spectators shook with laughter.
—The Republican-Courier, *November 28, 1911*

*O*ne of the most interesting and perhaps most misunderstood categories of crime for which perpetrators were arrested is that of violating game laws. The landscape in which the Gallatin Valley sits makes it a prime area for wild game and for the protection of these animals. The punishment for breaking game laws was harsh, including upward of $500 fines and/or jail time. Unfortunately, the stories behind many of these perpetrators are lost to time; however, looking at the time period and the season of the year, one can often surmise that the killing of game out of season or without a license was not always done with malicious intent. The Great Depression hit Montana roughly a decade before the rest of the nation, leaving many destitute and without means of adequately providing food for their families. Crime rates would rise and so would the violation of game laws, as fathers and husbands attempted to put food on the table. Looking through this lens, the killing of a deer in late November 1920, for example, may be seen as an act of desperation. Add to the act a $500 fine or months of jail time, and one can see the way in which these laws negatively affected a portion of the population. In April 1910 it was noted that 46,431

Elk hunt in Gallatin Canyon, circa 1900. *Gallatin Historical Society/Gallatin History Museum.*

hunting and fishing licenses had been granted in Montana that year, $1 per license for those living in the state, $25 per license for those out of state. Alien licenses were issued to non–U.S. citizens for $10 each. To put these numbers in perspective, $1 in 1910 would be equivalent to $27 today. The average household in 1910 made less than $600 a year. Within a few years, by 1917, alien gun laws would take away arms from anyone who was not a U.S. citizen, leaving those who used legal hunting as a means of survival without means to take wild game. While this does not condone the offenses of hunting out of season or without a license, it does give one a better perspective as to why many chose to run the risk of offending the law.[120]

In 1912, a new game preserve was established in the area, with rules that needed to be outlined so offenders would know which side of the law they were on. For example, if a hunter wounded an elk outside of the preserve, but the elk strayed inside to die, the hunter could finish his elk and, with the help of game wardens, remove it from the area. This was unlike the Yellowstone National Park boundary, where the line was solid: once an animal crossed, it was unreachable by the hunter.[121]

A story both humorous and a little sad centers on local attorney John A. Luce, who unwittingly found himself standing before the bar of justice not in defense of someone else, but in the position of his usual clients, as the accused. Luce had bagged a pheasant up Bridger Canyon and showed it to the worst possible person, whom he happened to bump into on Main Street later that day: the game warden. He proudly introduced his "dandy bird" to the man, to which the warden replied, "And I suppose your buggy ran over and killed it." Luce was forced to plead guilty, as he could not afford to pay for legal advice, and he was leniently fined fifty dollars for the crime. According to the paper, all Luce had to say in his defense was that he had done the deed, but he wished to inform the judge, "It was a great shot that brought it down—a shot to be proud of." A deputy responded, "Possibly so, but I don't think you'll be so proud of it when I tell you it will prove the costliest bird you ever killed," to which, as the paper put it, "the spectators shook with laughter."[122]

There were also those who clearly were sidestepping the law by throwing sticks of dynamite in lakes and ponds to kill as many fish as possible, as quickly as possible. There were five arrests for this offense, one in 1912, after which Antonio Styongo found himself "languishing" at the jail. He would be committed to a trial, the outcome of which is unknown. Styongo used a charge on the waters of Sixteen Mile Creek that May and was caught by Deputy Game Warden Henry Ferguson.[123]

There are many other outlying crimes listed in the ledgers, including gambling and blackmail. One interesting character booked at the Gallatin County Jail is Overton Tudor. He was first booked on May 6, 1912, for gambling; the fine for this offense cost him seven months' imprisonment at the jail and a fine of $500, although an appeal in the case seemed imminent.[124] Overton would be arrested three times on three separate crimes. His second stint at the jail was January 26, 1915, for gaining money under false pretenses. It seems he did not serve time for either of these offenses. However, on March 20, 1917, he was booked for burglary, and although he was out on bond the same day, he was picked back up on a bench warrant on June 15, 1917, and sentenced to one year to thirty months in the penitentiary. It appears his time spent in Deer Lodge changed his outlook. Overton had been married in 1907 to a woman named Rebecca; together, they had six children. When she passed away in 1926, it seems Overton moved in with his parents, passing away at age sixty-six; he was buried with his parents at Sunset Hills in Bozeman. From 1917 on, his record appears to be clean.

On June 16, 1938, Kyle Robert Podoll signed a statement describing his role in a blackmail scheme that took place in West Yellowstone. Kyle, along

Gear box for the presentencing cells. *Author's image.*

with Ray McCall, had conceived a "shakedown racket" for blackmailing local bars that were illegally conducting gambling. The plan was developed in Idaho, but the two boys were anxious about being known in the area, so they made their way to West Yellowstone. Before leaving Pocatello, however,

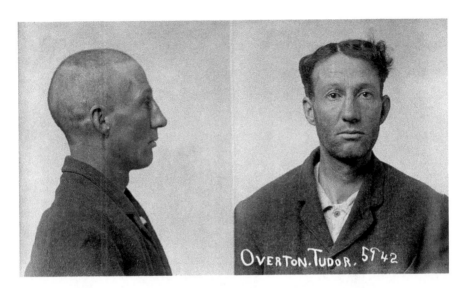

Overton Tudor, burglary first degree, 1917, prison, Deer Lodge, Montana. *Montana Historical Society.*

they stole, on a few separate occasions, four 10-pound cases, five 25-pound cases and three 50-pound cases of dynamite, as well as three 35-pound cases of electric blasting caps and a package of five hundred ordinary blasting caps. They planned to blackmail the bars with the threat of blowing them up if they did not comply with their demands. The boys found shelter at a cabin they knew, Albrecht's, near the town of West Yellowstone, before casing the area for potential victims. They decided on Doc's Place, John's Place, Bucy's Place and the Old Faithful Tavern as their targets. On the evening of June 13, they wrote out the extortion notes and packed four sticks of dynamite ready for use. The notes were as follows:

> *Dear Sir: Our Ass'n of Casino Owners will see that no more "unforeseen accidents" happen to your establishment for the nominal fee of $100.00 in $5 bills in a sealed white envelope this will entitle you to "protection" until August the 1st. This money will be called for between 7:30 and 8:00 pm Tuesday the 14th. Any attempt to evade or neglect immediate payment will result in complete destruction of your establishment within a week. Do not under any circumstances give the messenger any inkling of the nature of this transaction.*[125]

Tunnel connecting the jail with the Gallatin County Courthouse, constructed after 1938. It was used to transport prisoners from the jail to the courtroom. *Author's image.*

Kyle Podell, blackmail, 1938. *Montana State Prison records.*

West Yellowstone, 1976. *Gallatin Historical Society/Gallatin History Museum.*

Their first stop was Doc's, where Kyle planned to throw a lighted stick of dynamite on the roof. Upon arriving, however, they found the roof was slanted, which was not conducive to holding the stick. The dynamite was placed in a wood pile, instead. The plan had been to hit all the places on their list, but after the first, Ray became frightened, so the two dropped off the notes at the post office instead, where they heard the explosion from the stick they had left at Doc's. They then left town as fast as they could and returned to the cabin. In the explosion, one man—Arthur Clayton, age twenty-three—had been injured.

The next day, June 14, they went back into town, expecting to collect from the places to which they had sent the letters. It was Kyle's job to collect, while Ray waited in the getaway car. At the first stop, Doc's, he was given an empty envelope. The next stop was Bucy's, where he was to play fifty cents on the roulette wheel as an alibi. The plan was to state that a stranger had given him fifty cents to pick up these envelopes, if he was caught. While leaving Bucy's, he was taken into custody; the alibi clearly had not been ironclad enough. Ray, unsure what was happening to Kyle, didn't know what to do, so he stayed parked and took a nap until deputies came to his car and, having checked the license plate, brought him in as well. When Ray was asked by county attorney Landoe if his mother knew what was happening, he responded: "Yes....She's pretty well broken up about it, as she has a right to be."[126]

Kyle, age eighteen, would be charged with extortion, while Ray, age sixteen, would be tried in a juvenile court. According to Kyle's prison record, he served two years for blackmail and bombing property. It is unknown what sentence Ray was given.

Chapter 9

HORSES, JEWELS AND BACON

Grand Larceny, Robbery and Burglary

If a banker dumps his cash on tables outside his desk railings
and lets people handle it at will, he would not get much sympathy
when he complained that it had been stolen.
—*The* Weekly Avant Courier, *July 9, 1898*

*C*harges of grand larceny, burglary and robbery span the widest age
groups in the Gallatin County Jail records: the youngest offender was
eleven years old, and the oldest was eighty-eight. Out of 375 grand
larceny arrests, 88 were sent to the penitentiary, while out of 556 burglary
and robbery arrests, 119 were sent. Numerous accounts of petit larceny
were also listed. The distinct difference between burglary and robbery is
thus: burglary occurs when a person enters a place without consent and
takes items from that place, while robbery is when a person takes items from
another person in their presence using force or intimidation. Larceny is
when a person takes items without breaking into a place, such as stealing
from a publicly open store. The difference between grand and petit larceny
lies in the value of the items taken, which has changed over time, depending
on inflation.

Early in 1898, Harry Patterson had quite the scare while leaving a dance
party at the Armory Hall. While passing through the alley between the
Gallatin Mercantile Company and the Courier Office, he was held up with
force. It seems the man heard a noise and, before he could turn all the way
around to see what had caused it, was hit by something like a billy club

The Hold-up.

Drawing made of the "Hold-up" by newspaper staff. *Avant Courier*, February 19, 1898. *Gallatin Historical Society/Gallatin History Museum.*

before he had a chance to brace himself. The robber got away with only a few small coins, but Patterson was left with a nasty bruise across his cheek. It was noted that the perpetrator would probably not be caught, as Patterson had been unable to get a good look at him. The most interesting part of this occurrence, perhaps, is the crude drawing that was made for the paper detailing the event. A caption read: "It seems a paradox to say a man is 'held up' when a fellow knocks him down and holds him down, too, while going through his pockets. But such is really the case, as the above illustration shows. For obvious reasons, the features are disguised."[127]

On April 18, 1898, the Golden Rule store (later to be known as Chambers-Fisher) was broken into during the night, while two clerks slept upstairs. The goods were found at Mrs. Carrington's house, along with items missing from other burglaries. Mrs. Carrington was arrested but soon released, while her two sons E.H. Burlingham and Emmet L. Burlingham were taken into custody for the multiple burglaries. Little is known about their sentencing; however, E.H. had been arrested at age nineteen in 1896 for grand larceny and had spent time at a reform school.

Interior of the Chambers-Fisher Co., 1972. *Gallatin Historical Society/Gallatin History Museum.*

Later that year, in July, the *Weekly Avant Courier* would print a short article on shoplifting. The author condemned the methods by which modern department stores were displaying their wares for anyone to just pick up. This was a relatively new technique, as compared to the previous system of having everything behind counters, where a clerk would assist the buyer with the goods. According to the author:

> *If a banker dumps his cash on tables outside his desk railings and lets people handle it at will, he would not get much sympathy when he complained that it had been stolen, and if he continued the practice because these losses were more than offset by the increased profits which the displays resulted in, as is the case with the department stores, there would be much justice in the claim that he had no right to make profits by any method which tended to debauch the public. In short, it may fairly be maintained that it is a prime duty of every citizen to exercise reasonable diligence in safeguarding his own property, and that if he neglects this he becomes in a measure a menace to society.*[128]

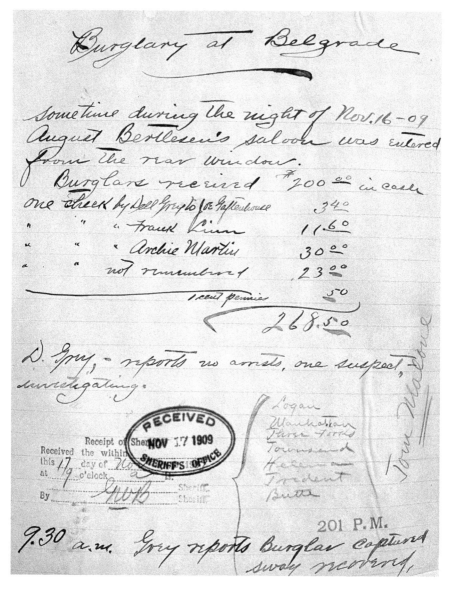

Notes on a burglary at Belgrade, 1909. *Gallatin Historical Society/Gallatin History Museum.*

In November 1932, two women, Mable Peace, age twenty-four, and Margaret Blevins, age thirty-two, were arrested for shoplifting. Police were alerted to the women after reports from Chambers-Fisher, Montgomery Ward, J.C. Penney and the George McCracken store that items had been stolen. The merchants were all able to give descriptions of the two women.

At first, they denied having anything to do with the stolen items, and in fact, Margaret refused to give her name. The women had registered at the Fleming Hotel as M.L. Hodges and her sister from Missoula. When their room was searched, silk stockings, dresses and lingerie worth a total of $300 were discovered, all matching the descriptions of the items stolen from the stores. When the women broke down and confessed, they stated that they needed money and had intended to sell the items. They claimed this was their first offense of this kind. According to the women, they had found it "so easy to steal the merchandise" that it was "impossible to resist the temptation." It seems the car in which the women were traveling, with Washington plates, might not have been their own, as they were unable to provide ownership documentation.[129]

A week later, the women were pleading "not guilty" to a charge of grand larceny, due to their assertion that the value of the items was under fifty dollars. According to reports, they were being charged by county attorney Fred Lay with stealing fifty-five dollars' worth of merchandise from the Chambers-Fisher Company. It is unknown why they were not being held accountable for the other stolen goods. However, by this time, Butte had got wind of their arrest, and the department was asked to hold them in case they were not convicted in Bozeman, so they could be tried in Butte for the theft of a mink coat from Hennesty in Butte. By this time, it had come out that Margaret Blevins had several aliases, and this was not her first offense. Under the name of Tillie Pence, she had served time in the penitentiary at Walla Walla, Washington, on a grand larceny charge. It seems she had quite a career in the western states as a thief.[130] It is, unfortunately, not known what happened to the women. A search of newspaper articles for the months after their arrest proved unproductive, and the sentencing portion of the jail ledger remains empty.

The following year, in April 1933, another two women would be accused of shoplifting; this time, their fate would be much more lenient. The women came from Helena to Bozeman, where they visited several stores, picking up items at each place. One of the women had a baby with her, which, according to the paper, they used "as a means of throwing off suspicion of their real purpose of visiting the stores." When they believed themselves unobserved, they would slip items into the baby's wrappings. The baby, however, would be their undoing. At George McCracken's store, the women had taken a few dresses from a display rack when a clerk came by the area. The women became frightened and hastened out, leaving behind the baby's bottle, which the clerk found suspicious. The women were followed to the

Tillie Pence, parole violation, 1926, Washington State Penitentiary. *Washington State Archives.*

Montgomery Ward store, where they went into a restroom. It was there that suitcases containing stolen merchandise were found. The items they had acquired were varied, from a can of paint and medicine to shoes, stockings, shirts, dresses and candy. Unlike Peace and Blevins of the year before, these women's pleas for leniency were granted. The women stated that they were very poor and had large families in Helena. They had hitchhiked to Bozeman to shoplift needed supplies. Once the items were returned, the merchants dropped any charges, and the women were secured transportation back to Helena by Sheriff Westlake.[131]

The 1900s saw an increase in both shoplifting, most likely due to this new method of display, and holdups. The latter would increase even more in the 1920s, as scenes of bank robberies in films gave young people big ideas. Highway robbery had been common along the various trails out West, as it was relatively easy to hold someone up at gunpoint at a turn in the road, where nobody would see the crime take place.

On July 11, 1912, one such highway robbery took place that one could find rather humorous. Two young boys about ten to twelve years of age held up William Flannery, a rancher who lived along the East Gallatin Road. On his way into town, on the edge of the city, the two boys stepped out from behind some machinery with six-shooters in their hands, thrusting them into his face. Flannery was, at the time, unable to determine the type of guns the boys had but believed they might be toy guns. He believed this enough to continue forward, despite their continued pursuit. As of the writing of the article detailing these events, Deputy Del Gray had not located the boys. It was assumed that the boys had not been serious in their robbery attempt but had gotten their plan from some "lurid literature." It was apparent, however, that were they to be located, a punishment would be imminent.[132]

Another group of boys was not as lucky. In 1912, four young men, ages seventeen to twenty, were arrested for stealing chickens from Mrs. J.J. McCay. A local chicken fancier also stated that over one hundred of his hens had been stolen, but those crimes could not be laid on the boys. They were each fined ten dollars, and it was believed that the cases of chicken thievery in the town would drop considerably with this punishment.[133]

It was also during this time that more people began traveling from the mid-East out to the West Coast. The Yellowstone Trail was conceived in 1912 as an automobile route that cut across the United States, running through the area of Bozeman. This influx in through traffic, along with those traveling by rail, led to an increase in burglary and robbery, particularly along the rail stops and road routes. On July 16, 1912, an article in the *Republican-Courier* mentioned a robbery at Trident in which $100 was taken out through a side

Telegram from Laurel, Montana, to the Gallatin County Sheriff's Department, asking for the whereabouts of a runaway boy. 1909. *Gallatin Historical Society/Gallatin History Museum.*

Short train traveling along the Gallatin River, east of Logan, circa 1918. *Gallatin Historical Society/Gallatin History Museum.*

window of the post office. It was noted that orders had been sent around to "pick up and search all tramps found anywhere near the railroads in the county." According to the paper, four iceboxes in town had been burgled, and chicken, beer and cheese had been taken. A paper sack with the remains of this lunch had been found near Logan.[134]

In fact, the term "tramp" began to be used frequently in the papers during this time to label any transient-like individual. They would be most often targeted as the perpetrators of crimes, sometimes unfairly singled out and sometimes rightly so, as in a case from 1911. Albert Heiser, a young shipping clerk, was knocked down from behind near the railway tracks by Logan, beaten senseless and robbed of all his belongings. His assailants were in the act of deciding how to deal with the young man permanently when they were heard by A. Herzog, a section foreman, who had been sleeping nearby in the brush. The men attacked Herzog, cutting his hands and arms, but he managed to escape, and his cries for help startled the men into running away, as they were heard by others. The men were discovered at the river, attempting to swim across; however, two of the men could not swim, and thus they were all caught and brought to shore at the point of a Winchester. Young Albert Heiser had been miraculously saved.

What Herzog had witnessed the assailants discussing was undoubtedly the demise of the young clerk. According to Herzog, one of the men had been for placing the tied and gagged Heiser on the railway tracks, while two of the men argued that they should tie a rock around Heiser's neck and throw him in the river. If it had not been for Herzog's cries, the latter plan was going to be carried out. It was believed that one of the men, Williams, was going to plead guilty, shouldering the blame, while the other two would put up a legal fight. All three of the men were found to be from the Puget Sound area and all underage.[135]

In the end, all three of the "tramps," George Williams, Guy Bonners and Claude Cosman, received a sentence of five years at the state penitentiary. It came out at the trial that Heiser had known the men, and they had been traveling together. The judge moved toward leniency and recommended each sentence be cut down if the men remained on good behavior at the prison. The case brought considerable interest, and the courtroom was packed for most of the trial.[136]

That same year, in January 1911, the sheriff's office made a capture that, according to the *Republican-Courier*, "would do justice to the brain of Sherlock Holmes." Marion J. Davis and Glenn Henderson were caught by Undersheriff George Battenfelder after a month of day-and-night investigation. On the morning of December 2, 1910, the pair had burglarized the Logan post office—amazingly enough, with the clerk, Henry Morrison, asleep only four feet from the money drawer. The clerk had not awakened when a loud alarm bell on the till went off. The loss was not discovered until the clerk got up at six o'clock that morning. The only clue to the perpetrators' identities was a letter that one of them men had accidently dropped. It was addressed to a man in Spokane and signed "Bertha." With hard investigation, it was discovered that the letter had been written by a girl in Livingston and given to a man named Glenn Henderson for delivery. His failing to do so in a timely manner ended up being the team's undoing. It was believed that the men had gone to Washington, and from thence aid was requested, but it seems the Washington authorities were indifferent to the matter.[137]

It soon came out that Henderson had a "sweetheart" in Livingston, which prompted local authorities to begin scanning the mail for any correspondence from the man to his girl. Several letters were discovered, including, finally, one that detailed where the girl should send some packages Davis and Henderson had left behind. Within hours, Sheriff Sales and post office inspector Albert Paisley were on a train headed for Concrete, Washington. There, the sheriff of Skagit County helped make

Collection of locks from burglaries donated by the Law and Justice Center. *Image by Victoria Richard.*

the arrest of Henderson and Davis. The two were returned to Bozeman. Davis was thirty-two years of age and believed to be an ex-convict, while Henderson was nineteen. The latter would be the first to confess to the burglary. From the Logan post office, the two men had taken $80 and two revolvers. It seems they had previously robbed the post office in Monarch, Wyoming, of $139 in cash, $100 in jewelry and some clothes.[138]

According to the jail ledger, the two were booked as Johnathan Davis, age thirty-two, and Henry Henderson, age nineteen, but in follow-up articles about the case, they are referred to as L.M. Davis and Glen W. Henderson. Henderson would be released by the court due to his confession and age. Davis, however, would receive five years. According to Henderson, Davis, whom he knew as "Cassidy," had done the burglary, while he had stood watch. Davis had not told him about the money he had taken, just the two revolvers, which they pawned.[139] There is a Glen Henderson in the state

Train depot at Logan, Montana. *Gallatin Historical Society/Gallatin History Museum.*

penitentiary records, age nineteen; however, the document states the charge was grand larceny in Townsend in November 1911. This could be the same "Glenn Henderson" described in the papers related to the Logan robbery, or it could be a coincidence.

On July 21, 1915, a letter was written on Deer Lodge State Prison paper from C.C. Skidmore, Box #7, to Mr. Del Gray, Bozeman, Montana. The letter contains an apology from Skidmore to Sheriff Del Gray and a plea for assistance in obtaining parole. In the letter, Skidmore writes: "You gave me some good advice as I see it now and I thank you for it although it was found out [too] late….I would like to hear from you and know your disposition in matter of my getting release." This plea for help prefaces a file full of letters back and forth between law enforcement departments across Montana with regards to stolen Ford cars, followed by a mass of telegrams asking witnesses for appearances in the courtroom reaching as far as California.

Partway through the story, a Mr. and Mrs. I.C. Petrie enter the mix, arrested in Dillon for driving a stolen car out of Bozeman. It seems on July 11, 1917, two Ford cars were stolen in Bozeman, at Al G. Barnes's showgrounds near the Northern Pacific Depot. Three days later, Skidmore was arrested after shipping two casings from the express office of the depot to an I.C. Petrie in Butte, Montana. One car was soon found in a barn rented by Skidmore and was identified by the owner, despite the numbers having been worked over and changed. The casings found in Butte matched

C.C. Skidmore, grand larceny, 1917, Gallatin County Jail. *Gallatin Historical Society/Gallatin History Museum.*

the original numbers of the owners' car, as sold to the rightful owner by the Story Motor Supply Co. The Petries had, by that time, headed to Dillion, but officers discovered a photo album in their room that gave them positive identification of the couple.[140]

While the Petrie car was not the second stolen car, it was most likely another stolen car. It seems the little group had a full racket going. On June 27 of that year, they had offered a Ford car for sale in the *Bozeman Chronicle*, which they had sold successfully. Mrs. Petrie claimed to know nothing about stolen cars, stating that Skidmore had presented himself as a man trying to stay out of sight of a girl, hence all the secrecy while doing business dealings. It appears the sheriff's office did not believe this story. Skidmore did have a rap sheet that included grand larceny and assault charges, but the way in which the Petries sold the cars anonymously in the papers raises a question as to their innocence in the matter. According to the *Weekly Courier*, Mrs. Skidmore had come to her son's aid, stating that they had traveled to Montana for his health. She had taken a trip to Seattle, leaving her son in Butte, and returned to learn of all the trouble he had gotten into. It was noted that "all the members of the party were very well addressed and appear to be persons of culture and refinement."[141]

On November 7, 1917, it was announced that Skidmore had been found guilty of grand larceny. Mr. Petrie's trial was to follow the next day, at which he, too, was found guilty. Skidmore would receive a sentence of four and a half to nine years and Petrie three to seven years. Their prison intake papers list Skidmore's occupation as auto mechanic and photographer and Petrie's as electrician lineman and barber. Nothing was said about Mrs. Petrie, who did not serve time for her part in the scheme.[142] It is also unknown what became of the group once their sentences were up. Their names have not been able to be traced.

Perhaps one of the most colorful notations in the jail records is that of the arrest of Ed Long, Joe Ford and Harvey Jensen. They were booked on February 20 and 21 for grand larceny: "stealing bacon." All three were originally sentenced to Deer Lodge under terms of twelve to eighteen months, fifteen to thirty-five months and eighteen months to four years, respectively. However, on April 28, 1930, Ed Long appealed to the court and was tried and found not guilty, but he would not stay out of trouble for more than a year. On June 26, 1931, Ed Long pled guilty for having robbed the Gallatin Gateway Supply of a rifle, ammunition and blankets in October with Harvey Jensen. There is not a notation as to what happened to Ed Long after his guilty plea, but his name wasn't found in state penitentiary records, so it is possible that he was lucky enough to escape a prison sentence yet again.[143] There is a Joseph Ford listed in the Deer Lodge records for burglary crimes committed in the Bozeman area, but there is not an intake paper for

I.C. Petrie, grand larceny, 1917, Gallatin County Jail. *Gallatin Historical Society/Gallatin History Museum.*

the 1930 grand larceny charge, so either he didn't serve time for that crime, or there is another Joe Ford missing in the records.

Harvey Jenson is another story. He was first booked into the Wisconsin State Reformatory for grand larceny on a term of one year. He was released on May 5, 1926, and made his way to Montana. On May 20, 1927, he was booked in Deer Lodge for first-degree burglary and sentenced for two to four years. Following this second arrest in 1927, his wife filed for a divorce in Gallatin County, taking custody of their two children. He gained parole on May 20, 1929. Harvey would serve time—unlike Long and Ford, who both managed to appeal and avoid their sentences—for the meat market burglary, during which, it is noted in his prison record, he had stolen "some bacon." Shortly following his discharge on April 27, 1931, he would be again sent to Deer Lodge for the Gallatin Gateway Supply burglary he conducted with Ed Long. His sentence would be for one year, which he served until February 25, 1932, when he was discharged. Again, his freedom would be short-lived, as he was booked again on April 21, 1933, on another burglary charge in Reedpoint, Stillwater County. This time, the sentence was for five years.[144]

Gallatin Gateway. *Gallatin Historical Society/Gallatin History Museum.*

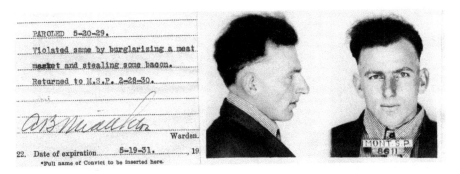

PAROLED 5-20-29.

Violated same by burglarizing a meat
market and stealing some bacon.

Returned to M.S.P. 2-28-30.

Warden.

22. Date of expiration............5-19-31..............., 19
Full name of Convict to be inserted here.

Harvey Jensen, burglary first degree, 1930, prison, Deer Lodge, Montana. *Montana Historical Society.*

Food goods were the subject of two burglaries that occurred on the same evening in October 1932. It seems J.W. Whit of West Yellowstone had packed up his grocery store in boxes to move to Ashland, Idaho, then left to go get a truck. Upon his return, he found nearly all the stock had been stolen, including 490 pounds of flour, 100 pounds of sugar, 40 pounds of lard, a case of mixed spices and a case of canned goods, as well as cases of butter, eggs, soap and all the tobacco and cigarettes. That same evening, across the county in Central Park, burglars broke through a window at the Central Park Creamery, escaping with 52 rounds of 23-pound cheese. Wilber Curtis, E.E. Snow and a man named Freman would be arrested on the twentieth of October for burglarizing the Schneider Cheese Factory of 30 cakes of cheese. This must have been related to the Central Park burglary in some way. [145]

Also in 1932, Irl Sievert, age twenty-one, was arrested for attempting to burglarize the Sawyer store. An alarm sounded, which had notified the police of the ongoing theft. The man had intended to steal winter clothing. He was held at the city jail, where, pending his hearing, he attempted to hang himself with his belt. Patrolman Ralph Richards had, luckily, passed into the area where Sievert was being held and found him hanging just in the nick of time. The man was unconscious but not severely injured. Suffocation had been sure to ensue, however, had Richards not stepped in. At Sievert's hearing, he entered a plea of guilty, stating that the humiliation of arrest had prompted him to try to take his own life. Following sentencing, he was moved to the county jail under a $750 bond. [146] Sievert had been married that May to Lena Ellen Callantine. It appears he received a two-year suspended sentence and lived to be seventy-eight years of age.

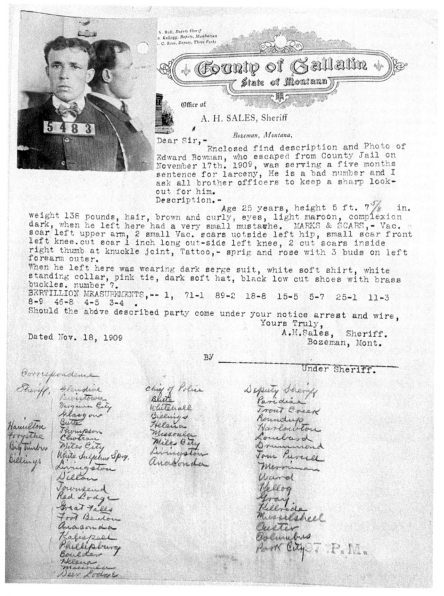

Letter to local sheriffs detailing an escaped convict from the Gallatin County Jail: Edward Bowman, larceny, 1909. *Gallatin Historical Society/Gallatin History Museum.*

In December 1932, A.W. Clampett was arrested on a grand larceny charge for burglarizing the Lovelace Grocery Company of $700 worth of cigarettes. At his trial, the accused told a rather sensational story. According to Clampett, the only witness called by the defense, he had been retained by

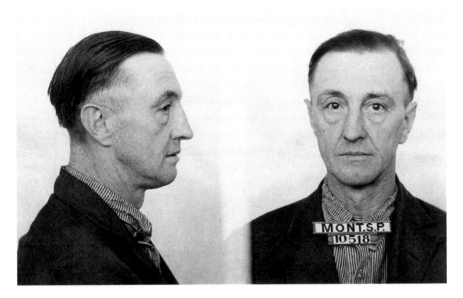

A.W. Clampett, grand larceny, 1932, prison, Deer Lodge, Montana. *Montana Historical Society.*

four men, all strangers to him, to take liquor to Billings. When he arrived to load up the goods, he quickly realized the boxes did not contain liquor. When he protested the situation, one of the men "shoved a gun against his side, threatening to kill him if he did not go through with them." He was to be paid twenty dollars for the delivery. The trip was made to Billings that night. On the way, two cases of the cigarettes were cached in Rocky Canyon, while the rest were delivered to Billings. Clampett was given his twenty dollars and had a drink with the men before they all departed and were not seen by Clampett again. He stated he was in no way connected with the robbery. It was testified that men had been seen loading the boxes. In that respect, Clampett had been telling the truth: there had been other men present. However, the rest of his story seems not to have been believed, as his next home became the state penitentiary, where he would serve two and a half years.[147]

A rather humorous incident occurred when George Robinson was hired to break a colt for A. Harkinson in Manhattan in 1910. It was noted that after "riding the animal for a couple of days horse saddle, bridle and Robinson disappeared." It was thought that the rider had headed toward Sedan near the Gallatin County boundary, leading Sheriff Sales and Deputy Battenfelder to ride all night through a blizzard in pursuit. They

George Robinson, grand larceny, 1910, prison, Deer Lodge, Montana. *Montana Historical Society.*

caught the man and brought rider and horse back to Bozeman. Robinson was nineteen years old at the time and would spend the next year at the Deer Lodge Prison.[148]

Another crime of opportunity happened in November 1910, when George Wilson, while a clerk at Steffins's jewelry store, left town with a valuable watch charm and diamond ring, which C. Rose had brought into the store. At the time that the jewelry was received, Wilson was in the shop but off duty, thus clearing the shop of responsibility in the matter, according to the paper.[149]

Valuable jewelry was the subject of a case in 1912, in which $1,500 worth of jewels were stolen from a Miss Lillie Adams at a Three Forks resort. Among the jewels was a turquoise-set ring containing five stones and a circle of thirty-one stones, valuing $550 alone. Four men were immediately brought into the jail for examination. It doesn't appear that the jewels were recovered or the thieves apprehended.[150]

In 1932, robbers held up the Baltimore Hotel, then made good their escape. No arrests appear in the ledger books that seem to relate to this crime. The two men, who were unmasked, entered the hotel at three o'clock in the morning. When Ed Cass, night clerk, came up from the basement, where he had been working on a furnace, he found the men standing near a cigar case. When he approached them, they both raised six-shooters at him and told him to "stick 'em up." The robbers left with $31.90 from the cash register and $25 from Cass, whom they had physically searched for money. The police and sheriff were immediately notified, and Cass could give a good description of the two men, who had been about forty-five and thirty years of age. However, it seems when the robbers stepped out into the alley, they simply vanished.[151]

Chapter 10

"I AM TRYING TO GET OUT"

Escapes from Jail

Their tracks were plainly discernable in the snow this morning.
They went to the corner of Mendenhall and Third and dispersed from there.
It is believed some of them caught outgoing trains.
—*The* Evening Courier, *December 22, 1911*

he earliest jail escape in Bozeman was in 1873, conducted by Charles Clay, who was confined for attempting to kill Constable Holt. At the writing of the *Courier*'s tale, it was unknown who Clay's accomplice had been, but it was evident there had been one. According to Clay, who was eventually recaptured, he had found an old file in the jail, which he used to remove his shackles. He used the handle of his cup to open the lock and escape. However, upon scrutiny, it was determined that the shackles had been filed by a brand-new instrument, and the spring in the lock had been broken. Clay had also been found to have money on him when he was recaptured, of which he had had none while he was in jail. Clay's whereabouts had been mistakenly discovered by a herd of cattle. It seems Deputies Thomas Lewis and C.L. Clark had noticed a group of cattle looking at a straw stack, as though someone was there. The deputies soon apprehended Clay, using the persuasive argument to come out and give himself up or they would shoot. It was noted that the county commissioners had refused to supply funds to construct a fence around the jail: "A penny wise and pound foolish." It seems the cost of the search had cost more than the fence would have.[152]

The old city hall, jail, fire department and opera house, before it was razed in 1966. *Gallatin Historical Society/Gallatin History Museum.*

An attempt had been made two years previously, in 1871, but had been intercepted. Two prisoners, who were awaiting transfer to the state penitentiary, were discovered to have procured a case knife from outside, which they had turned into a saw. When Sheriff Guy went in to prepare the men for the transfer, it was discovered that the bars of the door had been sawn almost in two.[153] When Sheriff Blakely conducted a search of the jail in 1883, he discovered among the prisoners two saws constructed from knives, a saw frame and a bottle of strong acid, and he found that a bolt was missing from one of the cells. Blakely discovered these tools in the cell of a man who had committed murder in Rocky Canyon. The jail was assigned extra security personnel, and continued searches were conducted.[154] In May 1873, James B. Finch created a "massive" lock for the jail that would "successfully resist all efforts of prisoners to get out of jail, as well as prevent mobs from effecting an entrance."[155] While the mobs would end (such as the one that resulted in the lynching of Triplett and St. Clair, in February of that year), the escapes would be far from over.

William Brown, held for horse stealing, made his escape on the night of May 28, 1878. Brown used a method that would become a fairly common practice at the building. He managed to take up the floor in a vacant cell and sink a shaft about four feet deep, then sideways, under the jail wall. The soil from his "mining operations" was stored in a water closet, where it would not be discovered. It was clear Brown had carried out his work over a considerable amount of time. Just one year previously, county commissioners had installed an iron cell at an expense of $4,000; unfortunately, Brown had not been placed in it.[156]

On August 2, 1879, two prisoners, McCarty and Fox, cut a hole in the floor of the jail and escaped by burrowing their way through the foundation. Fox, who was in for larceny, having stolen jewelry from a party in east Bozeman, was recaptured two days later. McCarty, in for burglarizing John Potter's store in Hamilton, was still on the loose but had been spotted more than once.[157]

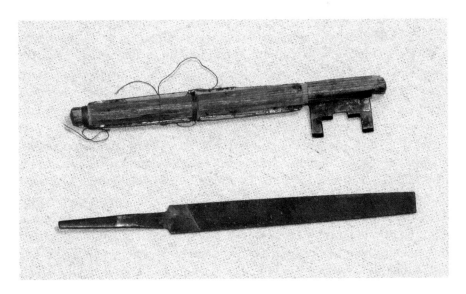

Makeshift key and a file confiscated from prisoners. *Image by Victoria Richard.*

Main Street Bozeman, circa 1980s; the Laclede Hotel stands at right. *Gallatin Historical Society/Gallatin History Museum.*

Shortly after his capture, Fox intimated a connection with Phillip Skeehan, landlord of the Laclede Hotel, suggesting Skeehan was complicit in the escape. Skeehan was quickly arrested, to the astonishment of the town, who believed the man to be of enviable reputation. By all accounts, it seems the community was right in their assessment of the man, as the case against Skeehan was dismissed on insufficient evidence. Fox had spoken only to a night guard, confidentially, and would not repeat his inferences under oath. It seems the arrest of Skeehan had been a grave mistake.[158]

In May 1884, Joe Didawick, a guard at the county jail, discovered an attempted escape, alerted to the proceedings by unusual noises. Upon inspection, it was found that the iron grating in a little anteroom toward the west side of the building had been forced open enough to nearly admit a person. An alarm was sounded, and a search was made of the jail yard, while an armed guard was put on watch at the opening, with instructions to shoot anyone who emerged. The prisoners were rounded up, and it was found that all were accounted for. The opening had been created with an axe near the window frame, where the sill had been broken in two and enough stone removed to allow the iron grating to be pried to the side.

Those perpetrating the deed were within five minutes of gaining freedom. It seems the axe had been handed in through the grating by a person who had access to the jail yard. It was noted that upon the wall of the closet was written "$22,000 reward is offered," showing that those attempting the escape had thought their success a sure bet.[159]

In 1885, two more escapes were attempted. In March, the escape of Patsy Burns (alias Edward Biggs) and a man named Bryant was discovered by Jailer Wilbur, who had come across blankets and a plank near the jail wall, placed in a way that hinted at escape. Burns was in for several charges, including gambling, while Bryant was awaiting trial for the murder of a man named Bowman in Livingston the previous December. Burns was found on the Bridger Canyon Road and seemed "heartily glad to return"; however, it is unknown if Bryant was ever found.[160] Burns would be taken to Deer Lodge for a term of two years.

The second escape in July was perpetrated not at the jail but at the county hospital. A man known as "Jandos, the incorrible [*sic*]" had taken ill while at the jail and been conveyed to the hospital. While there, he made his escape and returned to his wife in Timberline. He was promptly rearrested and, with much difficulty, brought back to Bozeman, with the help of the train men.[161]

These escapes were followed by a string of attempts—some successful, some not—from 1894 to 1903. On July 12, 1894, Thomas Keam, who was to serve seven years in the state penitentiary for highway robbery in Gallatin County, escaped along with three men being held for the sheriff of Silver Bow. They had dug a hole through the side of the jail wall and made it to Sixteen Mile Creek together, where they were discovered ready to embark on a handmade raft. Officers stationed themselves downstream, where Sheriff Caldwell called out to the fugitives to pull ashore—which they did without a fight and were taken back into custody.[162]

A year later, on July 30, two prisoners used a common table knife to cut a hole in the floor of the jail, thus gaining access to a space eighteen inches to two feet in height. In this space, they tunneled nine feet through the foundation, making their escape near the back steps of the courthouse into the courtyard. It was noted that their work had been "very fine" and that the trap door must have been carefully adjusted each morning, as no one ever saw anything amiss. Again, Sheriff Caldwell was on the search, but this time he came up empty-handed. There were no reports of a recapture, and the prisoners' names do not appear again in the jail records.[163]

Caldwell, Gallatin County sheriff from 1893 to 1897. *Gallatin Historical Society/ Gallatin History Museum.*

Again, the next year, on July 2, 1896, three prisoners made their escape; two remained at large, while one, Alex Cameron, was recaptured in Ennis, Madison County, after having stolen a horse from a man in Manhattan whom he had robbed previously.[164] On October 3, 1897, Maurice Flynn and August "Dutchy" Grube escaped by smuggling in a pick, digging their way through to a window and freedom. As these two men were in for somewhat minor offenses, and the evidence against them had not been all too sound, it was believed that a search would not be conducted to bring the men back to justice. According to the *Avant Courier*, it was "much cheaper" just to patch the hole in the wall than to search for the men and board them until their trials. It had been proposed to line the room with steel or iron to "break up these little sensational escapes which have been so frequent in the past years."[165]

The next several years went without a hitch, until 1903, when three escapes were made from the old jail. On May 3, Mike Ryan, jailed for having a valise and contents that were not his in his possession, dug through the jail wall with a penknife and his fingers. He had made a space just big enough to squeeze through. Ryan's escape would be unsuccessful, however; on June 6, he was booked at the jail with the crime "jail breaking," and within a month, he was sent to the Deer Lodge State Penitentiary for two years.[166] On September 19, Denis Downling, James Carter and James Blakely made their escape through a hole made by plumbers working on the courthouse. They had simply made the hole big enough to accommodate them while the jailer was away. The men were not found.[167]

The *Republican-Courier* of October 5, 1909, noted that the county jail was far too densely populated, extra space having been made to contain women, children and witnesses. It seems that the previous week, there had been twenty-three prisoners in one room. The sleeping areas were not sufficient for this number of people, thus forcing those incarcerated to take turns on the beds in shifts. According to the paper, "Most of the guests of the hotel Waldorf-Astoria de Sales" were serving short sentences for misdemeanors, with a few prisoners in the cage awaiting trials. The new jail that had been proposed that year had fallen through, due to a defect on the legal end, during

Museum construction, breaking through a wall of the jail to connect the sheriff's bedroom with the women's cells. *Gallatin Historical Society/Gallatin History Museum.*

which the county had been unable to sell bonds. It was believed the bonds would be voted on come the next election. It would not be until December 1911 that the county would see a new jail building ready to accommodate prisoners in an appropriate manner.[168]

On the morning of December 22, 1911, all were surprised to find that six prisoners had escaped from the brand-new $35,000 jail, which had been believed to be "escape proof."

The individual cells holding the prisoners were not locked, an oversight by the department, which believed the automatically locking front door to be adequate to hold the cell block.

The *Tacoma Times* of Washington would print a small article titled "Watchman Proved Good Sleeper," which was, in fact, partially true. Jailer Horace Bull was in the building, asleep in an overhead room, according to the *Bozeman Evening Courier.* According to the original blueprint, the jailer's office was located on the main floor, just a short distance from the cells. In this room, he probably would have heard some sort of commotion. But the article states he was "overhead," which means that he either was asleep in one of the unfilled portions of the building (women's cells, juvenile cells

Steam tunnel at the jail. *Author's image.*

or the infirmary) or in the sheriff's bedroom, which would have been on the opposite side of a two-foot concrete wall, with little chance of hearing anything going on in the cell block. This was clearly not an ideal situation for keeping watch over the prisoners, which goes to show the faith they had in the new locking mechanisms.

It seems the prisoners had made a point of studying these mechanisms as plumbers, painters and general workers came and went throughout the final stages of construction. In fact, the plumbers inadvertently had a helping hand in the escape, by leaving a tool kit behind with just the right instruments for the job of releasing the catch on the only door that kept the prisoners from the guard's corridor. As mentioned before, they were not locked into their individual cells.

The escape was far from over once access to the corridor was achieved. The group was still trapped in the cell block, with locked doors on all sides. However, they had a brilliant plan and, again, fateful means of execution. The workers had left behind a ladder. The prisoners climbed the grated cage of the bullpen and used the ladder to reach two small vent holes built into the north wall of the room. They used ropes made from blankets tied together to lower themselves into a narrow corridor. The corridor was part of the heating system for the building, allowing hot air pumped from the basement of the courthouse access to the new jail building. Beyond this corridor lay "Siberia," or the isolation cells. By all accounts, the corridor was a dead end, but somehow, the prisoners knew of the steam tunnel connecting the two buildings, which they used as their main objective. It is possible that one of the prisoners' experience as a boilermaker and machinist aided in the planning and execution of the escape.

At the east end of the corridor lay the tunnel, easily accessed by raising the grating covering the hole, which was about six feet deep. The tunnel itself was less than four feet tall, so the men had to crawl through it to the basement of the courthouse, where they found themselves trapped at the foundation of the courthouse. Armed with tools, however, the group managed to chip away and dig through this foundation, which led them to a little room below the treasurer's vault. Pushing through another floor grating, the men found themselves in the vault, with no way of escape, as the door was a locked iron barricade. Back in the room underneath, the group managed to break through another foundation wall, which led them into the boiler room. Once there, escape was easily achieved, and the men simply walked out of the building and into the city. The *Courier* noted: "Their tracks were plainly discernable in the snow this morning. They went to the corner of Mendenhall and Third and dispersed from there. It is believed some of them caught outgoing trains."[169]

Interestingly, there were other men locked into the bullpen that night, who did not have access to tools and were separated from the men in the cell block. Whether those escaping offered assistance to those still trapped is

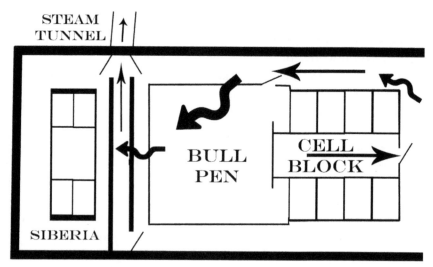

Scheme of the escape. *Author's image.*

unknown, but regardless, it seems the detained did nothing to try to alert the jailer, remaining relatively quiet throughout the ordeal.

The escapees were named and their arresting charges stated (not necessarily as accomplices to the same crime but charged with similar crimes): Fred Thompson and Ed Sayers, assault to commit robbery; Frank Furlong and George McCarrick, box car robbery; and Peter Mendeville and Joe Penna, burglary. It was noted that Thompson and Sayers were the "worst of the bunch," as they were the "thug type and dangerous."

The following day, the prisoners were still at large, although Sheriff Sales was quoted as saying, "They may have gotten out of Gallatin County, but they'll be caught sooner or later. We are working quietly on some clues." On January 1, 1912, three of the men were caught in Grand Island, Nebraska, nearly one thousand miles from Bozeman. Sheriff Sales himself made the trip to bring them back. The week before, Fred Thompson had been caught in Forsyth and brought back to Bozeman. According to the *Evening Courier*, upon Sheriff Sales's arrival in Forsyth, he found Thompson attempting yet another escape from the jail there, catching him in the act. The following week, Mendeville and Penna were still on the loose, but it was noted that the "dragnet is closing around them," and they could be caught any day. However, the search was quickly dropped, and the men were not pursued, in a "good riddance" gesture.[170]

For decades, this story has been shared with visitors to the Gallatin History Museum, formerly the 1911 county jail. A tunnel runs from the jail to the current courthouse, which is a delight to the many schoolchildren who tour the museum. The story was intertwined with this tunnel, which made perfect sense, until the 1911 article was read through, and the original blueprint of the building was revisited. Suddenly, the known tunnel did not make sense. The article mentioned a steam tunnel, and the blueprint had one noted, but it was at the northeast end of the building, not the southeast end. Then fate stepped in, just like it had for the escaping prisoners. During an exhibit change, a shelving unit was removed, and a hollow space was discovered under a portion of the flooring. After cutting through a section of plywood, the original steam tunnel was uncovered, and the story slipped right into place.

A piece of plexiglass was installed over the hole, so visitors can read the story and look down into the dingy basement where the prisoners made their escape. Today, a concrete wall barricades the entrance of the tunnel, as it would have run under the sidewalk to the courthouse, so one must imagine the open hole the prisoners managed to crawl through. But the new wall does give one an idea of the material the prisoners had to dig through to make their escape.

This would be the first of many escapes, but it certainly was the most embarrassing, occurring as it did immediately after the opening of the state-of-the-art jail.

A few years later, in 1913, J.P. Flaherity—who had been arrested for petty thievery conducted with Edward Ruey in Butte and Bozeman—was found within four inches of escaping the jail building. Using a table knife and fork, he had endeavored to dig a hole through the wall of the jail from a closet adjoining his cell upstairs. The two thieves had taken shirts from various stores and tried to sell them at the Northern Pacific railway station for fifty cents each. The two men had been separated so they could not communicate; thus, Flaherity was placed in an area not usually used by prisoners at the time. Undersheriff Mark Stout heard a slight scratching noise at three thirty in the morning and went in search of the cause; finding that the area where Flaherity was supposed to be was empty, he soon saw movement in the closet and demanded, "What are you doing there?" Flaherity calmly replied, "I am trying to get out." The prisoner had been able create a hole about twenty inches across, fourteen inches high and fourteen inches deep; he had only one layer of brick left to remove to enact his escape when he was caught. Flaherity had hidden the debris in a blanket under his bed and used cloth to deaden the sound of the removal of the bricks and mortar. The prisoner was taken back downstairs to a steel cell, where he would remain confined until his sentencing with Ruey.[171]

Above: Wanted poster from the state prison at San Quentin, California, for Hubert P. Herr, grand larceny, in a collection of "wanted" memorabilia sent to and from the Gallatin County Jail. *Gallatin Historical Society/Gallatin History Museum.*

Opposite: Interior of the sheriff's room in the old Gallatin County Courthouse, pre-1911. *Gallatin Historical Society/Gallatin History Museum.*

In May 1914, Ross Maxwell and Alfred Botts attempted a jailbreak that ended poorly. It seems that Maxwell had carried two tiny steel saws into the building in the sole of one shoe. Over a number of days, the bars of the bullpen were sawn through with the small blades and the breaks covered with soap to evade detection. The bars were then pried apart one night, and the two men made it to the east wall, where they went to work on the brick, to no avail. They tried another wall but found it only led to another corridor, from which they could not escape (although this was the corridor where the first jailbreak in the building had occurred). Maxwell gave up the scheme and made his way back to the bullpen, leaving the older Botts behind. Botts, who walked with a limp, was unable to regain access to the bullpen, as Maxwell had fixed the bars back to their usual position. The next morning, jailer Huffman found Botts sitting in the corridor, and the whole story emerged. The two were placed in solitary confinement until their trials.[172]

Sometime on the night of December 7 or the morning of December 8, 1929, two boys held in the upstairs cells of the jail made their escape, leaving a third boy behind. Buster Pearson, age seventeen, had been booked for stealing W.O. Bohart's car in Livingston the month before. Orey Thurston and Alvah Fisher, ages sixteen and seventeen, respectively, had been brought in for breaking into Owenhouse Hardware in Belgrade in November. All were to receive a hearing on Monday. It seems from newspaper reports that

Left: Window frame in the women's bathroom, where Flaherity most likely made his escape attempt. *Author's image.*

Right: Bathroom of the women's cells, where prisoners attempted escapes in the 1911 jail. *Image by Victoria Richard.*

the boys were not held in the juvenile cells as they are marked on the blueprint plans of the jail. From the description provided, it seems the cells where they were kept were the women's cells. According to the *Courier*, the room was just above the offices facing Main Street, with the courthouse out the window to the side. This is the opposite side of the building from where the juvenile cells were located. Pearson and Thurston had used a quarter-inch rod taken from one of the beds to remove the window frame in the lavatory, then used the window weights as tools to remove the mortar, which had been soaked in water. A comforter had been used to deaden the sound of the brick removal. Fisher was apparently not involved, having slept through the whole ordeal. While a search began immediately for the two escapees, Fisher attended his hearing and received a suspended sentence on parole.[173]

On August 19, 1932, the *Bozeman Courier* reported the escape of J.H. Smith, who was being held on a robbery and assault charge along with three other men. Smith had been placed in the women's cells so that no communication could be made between him and the others. Sometime during the night,

J.H. Smith's escape route from the women's cells through one of the windows on the top floor. *Author's image.*

Smith managed to cut though two of the bars that covered the upstairs window and lower himself down with a rope made from a torn shirt. The department believed an accomplice had been at hand to supply Smith with the necessary tools and whisk him away. Ironically, the east side window was visible from Main Street and lit by the glare of a nearby lamppost. There were no further articles to give clues as to the outcome of Smith's escape, but it is worth mentioning that his name is not found in the prisoner registry again following his escape, leading one to believe he was not caught.

The following year, on September 17, 1933, Sheriff Lovitt I. Westlake discovered Edward Wilcox, who was being held on a rape charge, trying to escape the jail building. Wilcox had removed about a dozen bricks at the back of the building, using a screwdriver. He had covered up the hole he was making with a mattress, which he hung from a windowsill. When Sheriff Westlake discovered him, Wilcox still had two more layers of brick to go through to make his escape. Wilcox had started the attempt immediately following his arrest, making his way to the back of the jail through the door to the solitary confinement cells, which had been negligently left unlocked when the prisoners were let into the bullpen. The screwdriver had been given to the men to fix an electric stove but had not been removed from the area after this fix. According to Wilcox, he was planning to escape for his mother, as "it would break her heart if I was sent to prison." Wilcox had not planned

Men's presentence jail cells at the Gallatin County Jail, showing the shower stall, toilet and sink and cells. *Gallatin Historical Society/Gallatin History Museum.*

Painted wall where, legend has it, an escape attempt was made in the 1940s. It remains a mystery, despite evidence of damage to the outer wall of the jail building. *Author's image.*

to escape right away; he was going to wait for the verdict at his hearing, and if convicted, he would use the hole he was hoping to have finished by that date. According to jail records, he was accused of raping a fifteen-year-old girl; however, at his hearing, he was tried and acquitted of the crime, making his attempted escape useless.[174]

In 1937, again under Sheriff Westlake, two men escaped from the jail. Fred Laurent, held for the theft of 473 skunk hides, and Fred Knabe, held for larceny and complicity in auto theft, used smuggled hacksaw blades to saw through the bars of the bullpen. They made their way to the ventilator shaft using an eyebolt, then sawed through a window to escape out the west side of the building.[175] Within days, the two men were recaptured and awaiting their respective trials. According to the *Chronicle*, when Undersheriff Isbell met back up with Knabe, he stated, "I expect I'm gladder to see you than anybody has ever been before," at which Knabe "wilted. Upon their return to the jail, they found they had become very unpopular residents. Stiffer discipline had ensued since their escape which led to the taking away of bullpen privileges for all."[176]

In 1982, Gallatin County received a new jail, known as the Law and Justice Center. The old brick building that had been the jail for over seventy years became the present-day Gallatin History Museum. Evidence of the escapes from this building can still be seen to this day, and new discoveries are often made, as the stories of those who spent time there are unearthed.

NOTES

Chapter 1

1. "Our County Jail," *Bozeman (MT) Avant Courier*, July 10, 1874.
2. "The Court House and Jail Site," *Bozeman (MT) Avant Courier*, September 11, 1879.
3. "Report of the Territorial Grand Jury," *Bozeman (MT) Weekly Chronicle*, January 7, 1885.
4. "November Term District Court," *Bozeman (MT) Weekly Chronicle*, November 16, 1887.
5. *Bozeman (MT) Weekly Chronicle*, August 29, 1883.
6. "How the County Is Run in Debt," *Bozeman (MT) Weekly Chronicle*, January 16, 1884.
7. *Bozeman (MT) Weekly Chronicle*, February 20, 1884.
8. *Bozeman (MT) Weekly Chronicle*, August 1, 1888.
9. "Vote for New Jail," *Republican-Courier* (Bozeman, MT), November 1, 1910.
10. "Total Cost New Jail Is $33,932.49," *Republican-Courier* (Bozeman, MT), January 9, 1912.
11. "Plans Are Ready for New Jail," *Republican-Courier* (Bozeman, MT), March 14, 1911.

Chapter 2

12. "Deer Lodge," *Bozeman (MT) Avant Courier*, March 29, 1877.

13. "Proposals," *Bozeman (MT) Avant Courier*, April 3, 1874.

14. "The News," *Bozeman (MT) Avant Courier*, September 20, 1877.

15. "Montana Condensed," *Bozeman (MT) Avant Courier*, September 4, 1879.

16. *Bozeman (MT) Avant Courier*, January 12, 1877.

17. "Telegraphic," *Bozeman (MT) Weekly Chronicle*, December 25, 1883.

18. "The 15th Legislature," *Bozeman (MT) Weekly Chronicle*, March 16, 1887.

19. "Sheriff's Sale," *Bozeman (MT) Weekly Chronicle*, September 15, 1886.

20. "John Stevens Dead," *Bozeman (MT) Weekly Chronicle*, June 1, 1887.

21. "City News," *Bozeman (MT) Weekly Chronicle*, October 7, 1885.

22. "Insanity—Its Causes," *Bozeman (MT) Avant Courier*, July 4, 1878.

23. "Why Farmer's Wives Become Insane," *Bozeman (MT) Avant Courier*, December 11, 1879.

24. "Variety," *Bozeman (MT) Avant Courier*, May 23, 1878.

25. "Great English Remedy," *Bozeman (MT) Weekly Chronicle*, August 15, 1888.

26. "Odds and Ends," *Bozeman (MT) Avant Courier*, May 30, 1878.

27. *Bozeman (MT) Weekly Chronicle*, January 7, 1885.

28. "A Victim of Insanity," *Bozeman (MT) Weekly Chronicle*, November 18, 1885.

29. "Insane Asylum," *Bozeman (MT) Weekly Chronicle*, April 15, 1885.

30. "Two Lunatics," *Bozeman (MT) Weekly Chronicle*, April 28, 1886.

31. "City News," *Bozeman (MT) Weekly Chronicle*, December 23, 1885.

32. "City News," *Bozeman (MT) Weekly Chronicle*, May 5, 1886.

33. "Evidently Insane," *Bozeman (MT) Weekly Chronicle*, December 15, 1886.

34. "McCann Released," *Bozeman (MT) Weekly Chronicle*, January 12, 1887.

35. "Montana Legislature," *Bozeman (MT) Weekly Chronicle*, March 2, 1887.

36. "Montana's Insane," *Bozeman (MT) Weekly Chronicle*, September 14, 1887.

37. "Tired of Life," *Bozeman (MT) Weekly Chronicle*, May 9, 1883.

38. "Cut His Throat," *Bozeman (MT) Weekly Chronicle*, January 6, 1886.

39. "Deputies Capture Dangerous Fugitive," *Republican-Courier* (Bozeman, MT), July 19, 1910.

40. Ibid.

41. "Willow Creek," *Bozeman (MT) Courier*, May 2, 1923.

42. "Worry Over an Imaginary Mortgage Causes Insanity," *Republican-Courier* (Bozeman, MT), January 30, 1912.

43. "Needless Worry Crazes and Kills," *Republican-Courier* (Bozeman, MT), February 13, 1912.

44. "Prohibition Brings Lower Death Rate in Treasure State," *Bozeman (MT) Courier*, December 12, 1923.
45. "Montana's Maniacs," *Bozeman (MT) Courier*, February 5, 1926.
46. "Mrs. Emil Felenzer Adjudged Insane," *Bozeman (MT) Courier*, July 18, 1923.
47. "List of Officers and General Information," *Bozeman (MT) Courier*, October 29, 1924.
48. "Neuman Speaks on Sterilization," *Bozeman (MT) Courier*, August 15, 1923.
49. "People Are Urged to Support Governor Dixon," *Bozeman (MT) Courier*, July 30, 1924.
50. "Ranch Hand Runs Amuck with Knife," *Bozeman (MT) Courier*, January 15, 1926.
51. "Insane Man to Warm Springs," *Bozeman (MT) Courier*, May 17, 1922.
52. "Kills Himself in County Jail," *Bozeman Daily Chronicle* (Bozeman, MT), July 24, 1924.

Chapter 3

53. "That the People May Know," *Bozeman (MT) Courier*, October 25, 1922.
54. "Sheriff's Force Makes Good Haul," *Bozeman (MT) Courier*, April 25, 1923; Prisoners Records, Gallatin History Museum, p. 4.
55. "Police Officers Destroy Booze," *Bozeman (MT) Courier*, May 9, 1923.
56. "Smith Takes 'Wild' Out of Roundup," *Bozeman (MT) Courier*, August 8, 1923.
57. "Captured Moon at Soft Drink Stand," *Bozeman (MT) Courier*, March 7, 1923.
58. "Deadly Copperas in 'White Mule,'" *Bozeman (MT) Courier*, January 9, 1924.
59. "Explosion Liquor Kills W.L. Ford," *Bozeman (MT) Courier*, 1932.
60. "Sheriff's Force Get Three Stills," *Bozeman (MT) Courier*, January 23, 1924.
61. "Hasty Officers Come Too Soon," *Bozeman (MT) Courier*, June 20, 1923.
62. "Mystery of the Missing 'Moon,'" *Bozeman (MT) Courier*, October 31, 1923.
63. "Sheriff Reports on Stills and Liquor Destroyed," *Bozeman (MT) Courier*, February 18, 1925.
64. "Insane Jealousy Prompts Rancher to Kill Wife and Attempt Suicide," *Bozeman (MT) Courier*, December 26, 1923.

65. Ibid.; "Sheriff's Force Get Three Stills," *Bozeman (MT) Courier*, January 23, 1924.
66. "Insane Jealousy Prompts Rancher to Kill Wife and Attempt Suicide," *Bozeman (MT) Courier*, December 26, 1923.
67. Prisoner Records, Gallatin History Museum, p. 26.
68. "Bozeman 'Leggers and Moonshiners Will Be Prosecuted in Police Court, Declares Magistrate M.R. Wilson," *Bozeman (MT) Courier*, November 12, 1926.

Chapter 4

69. Sheriff's Jail Record 1910–23, Gallatin Historical Society Archives.
70. "Waara and M'Vey Are Found Guilty," *Bozeman (MT) Weekly Courier*, June 5, 1918.
71. "Frank McVey Charged with Uttering Sedition," *Bozeman (MT) Weekly Courier*, April 17, 1918.
72. "Waara and M'Vey Are Found Guilty," *Bozeman (MT) Weekly Courier*, June 5, 1918.
73. "Two Men Are Sentenced to Prison for Sedition," *Montana Record-Herald* (Helena, MT), June 5, 1918.
74. Ancestry.com. U.S., World War II Draft Registration Cards, 1942 [online database].
75. Clemens P. Work, *Darkest before the Dawn* (Albuquerque: University of New Mexico Press, 2005).
76. "Sheriff Del Gray Starts Road Gang of Work Slackers," *Weekly Courier* (Bozeman, MT), June 12, 1918.

Chapter 5

77. "Fox, The Banker," *Bozeman (MT) Avant Courier*, September 12, 1878.
78. *Bozeman (MT) Avant Courier*, May 29, 1879.
79. "Helena Letter," *Bozeman (MT) Avant Courier*, August 14, 1879.
80. *River Press* (Fort Benton, MT), March 2, 1881.
81. "County Fund Shortage Sends Treasurer C. Corbly to Jail," *Republican-Courier* (Bozeman, MT), June 18, 1912.
82. Ibid.

83. "Corbly's Bond Is Fixed at $25,000," *Republican-Courier* (Bozeman, MT), July 2, 1912.
84. "Demurrer Filed in Corbly Case," *Republican-Courier* (Bozeman, MT), August 6, 1912.
85. "Clyde C. Corbly Released Upon Securing Bondsmen," *Republican-Courier* (Bozeman, MT).
86. "County Would Force Bondsmen to Pay Up," *Republican-Courier* (Bozeman, MT), February 26, 1913.
87. "Corbly Hears Witness Describe His Methods," *Republican-Courier* (Bozeman, MT), March 19, 1913.
88. "Judge Regrets Cannot Give Heavier Sentence," *Republican-Courier* (Bozeman, MT), March 26, 1913.
89. "Sentence of Year Is Given Young Embezzler," *Republican-Courier* (Bozeman, MT), January 21, 1913.
90. "Fake Company Exposed by Courier Two Years Ago," *Republican-Courier* (Bozeman, MT), March 5, 1912.
91. "Youth Aged 17 Thought to Be Smooth Forger," *Weekly Courier* (Bozeman, MT), July 16, 1913.
92. Ancestry.com, "Ned McAllister," Census, Prison and Death Records.
93. "Girl Check Writer Who Tried Suicide Now Happily Wed," *Billings Gazette* (Billings, MT) January 22, 1928.
94. "4 to 8 Years Is Forger's Penalty," *Bozeman (MT) Courier*, October 28, 1927.
95. "Man and Wife Are Held for Forgery," *Bozeman (MT) Courier*, July 25, 1930.
96. "Repeat Check Artist Gets Repeat Jail Seat," *Bozeman (MT) Courier*, July 28, 1944.

Chapter 6

97. "Maxwell Gets Two Years," *Avant Courier* (Bozeman, MT),
98. "Hold Two for Safe Blowing," *Weekly Courier* (Bozeman, MT), November 5, 1913.
99. "Local News," *Republican-Courier* (Bozeman, MT), November 29, 1910.
100. "Convicted of Adultery," *Weekly Courier* (Bozeman, MT), June 12, 1918.
101. "Disorderly House Raided by Police," *Bozeman (MT) Courier*, March 4, 1927.

102. "Obscene Career Ends by Capture," *Republican-Courier* (Bozeman, MT), April 16, 1912.
103. Ibid.

Chapter 7

104. "Alleged Bank Bandits Arrested in Sensational Raid at Havre," *Bozeman (MT) Courier*, December 5, 1923.
105. Ibid.
106. Ibid.
107. "Sheriff Jim Smith Finds Securities," *Bozeman (MT) Courier*, December 12, 1923.
108. "Sixteen Arrests of Yeggs Effected," *Bozeman (MT) Courier*, December 26, 1923.
109. "Montana County Sheriffs Clash with Burns Man in Bank Case," *Bozeman (MT) Courier*, February 20, 1924.
110. "Shortest Criminal Term of Court in Bozeman Closed Last Thursday," *Bozeman (MT) Courier*, March 5, 1924.
111. "Sheriff's Possee Kills Two Bandits in Gallatin Hills," *Bozeman (MT) Courier*, July 29, 1932.
112. Helen Backlin, interview with the author, March 15, 2021.
113. "Banks, Bullets, Bandits," *Bozeman (MT) Daily Chronicle*, September 19, 1994.
114. "Sheriff's Possee Kills Two Bandits in Gallatin Hills," *Bozeman (MT) Courier*, July 29, 1932.
115. "Curiosity Brings Crowds to Morgue," *Bozeman (MT) Courier*, July 29, 1932.
116. "Services for Bandits Today," *Bozeman (MT) Daily Chronicle*, July 29, 2932.
117. *Inmates of the Idaho Penitentiary 1864–1947* (Idaho Historical Society, 2008).
118. "Claim Reward for Dead Bank Bandit," *Bozeman (MT) Courier*, August 5, 1932.
119. "Banks, Bullets, Bandits," *Bozeman (MT) Daily Chronicle*, September 19, 1994.

Chapter 8

120. "Licenses to Fish and Hunt," *Republican-Courier* (Bozeman, MT), April 19, 1910.
121. "Bud Story Explains the Good of New Game Preserve," *Republican-Courier* (Bozeman, MT), January 2, 1912.
122. "John A. Luce Breaks Game Law Confesses, Is Arrested and Fined," *Republican-Courier* (Bozeman, MT), November 28, 1911.
123. "Jailed for Attempt at Dynamiting Fish," *Republican-Courier* (Bozeman, MT), May 14, 1912.
124. "Tudor Receives Heavy Sentence and a Fine," *Republican-Courier* (Bozeman, MT), May 14, 1912.
125. Affidavit, Kyle Podoll, June 15, 1938. *State Versus Kyle Podoll and Ray McCall.* Gallatin Historical Society.
126. "Statement of Raymond McCall," June 16, 1938, *State Versus Kyle Podoll and Ray McCall.* Gallatin Historical Society.

Chapter 9

127. "A Bold Hold Up," *Avant Courier* (Bozeman, MT), February 19, 1898.
128. "Shoplifting," *Weekly Avant Courier* (Bozeman, MT), July 9, 1898.
129. "Arrest Two Women Shoplifters Here," *Bozeman (MT) Courier*, November 4, 1932.
130. "Plead Not Guilty of Grand Larceny," *Bozeman (MT) Courier*, November 18, 1932.
131. "Shoplifters Raid Stopped by Clerk," *Bozeman (MT) Courier*, April 14, 1933.
132. "Fiasco Hold-Up by Boy Bandits," *Republican-Courier* (Bozeman, MT), July 16, 1912.
133. "Chicken Thieves Get Busy," *Republican-Courier* (Bozeman, MT), January 21, 1913.
134. "Robbers Capture $100 at Trident," *Republican-Courier* (Bozeman, MT), July 16, 1912.
135. "Brutal Tramps' Heinous Crime," *Republican-Courier* (Bozeman, MT), May 23, 1911.
136. "Tramps Convicted of Highway Robbery Receive Their Sentences," *Republican-Courier* (Bozeman, MT), June 6, 1911.

137. "Sheriff's Office Make Important Capture of Postoffice Robbers," *Republican-Courier* (Bozeman, MT), January 10, 1911.

138. Ibid.

139. "Logan Postoffice Robbers Convicted," *Republican-Courier* (Bozeman, MT), July 25, 1911.

140. Case files, Gallatin History Museum.

141. "Auto Thieves Are Landed by Local County Officers," *Weekly Courier* (Bozeman, MT), July 25, 1917.

142. "Skidmore and Petrie Taken to Deer Lodge," *Weekly Courier* (Bozeman, MT), November 14, 1917.

143. "Ed Long Pleads Guilty to Burglary Charge," *Weekly Courier* (Bozeman, MT), June 26, 1931.

144. Ancestry.com, "Harvey Jensen," Census, Prison and Divorce Records.

145. "Thieves Take All of Grocery Stock," *Bozeman (MT) Courier*, October 21, 1932.

146. "Despondent Thief Attempts Suicide," *Bozeman (MT) Courier*, November 11, 1932.

147. "Convict Clampett of Grand Larceny," *Bozeman (MT) Courier*, December 9, 1932.

148. "Local Briefs," *Republican-Courier* (Bozeman, MT), September 27, 1910.

149. "Wilson Is Brought Back from Seattle," *Republican-Courier* (Bozeman, MT), November 8, 1910.

150. "Valuable Rings Stolen in Three Forks," *Republican-Courier* (Bozeman, MT), March 12, 1912.

151. "Robbers Hold Up Baltimore Hotel and Make Escape," *Bozeman (MT) Courier*, August 12, 1932.

Chapter 10

152. "Jail Delivery," *Bozeman (MT) Avant Courier*, June 20, 1873.

153. "Local News," *Bozeman (MT) Avant Courier*, November 16, 1871.

154. "The City Chronicled," *Bozeman (MT) Weekly Chronicle*, May 16, 1883.

155. "Good Workmanship," *Bozeman (MT) Avant Courier*, May 23, 1873.

156. *Bozeman (MT) Avant Courier*, June 13, 1878.

157. "Jail Delivery," *Bozeman (MT) Avant Courier*, August 7, 1879.

158. "Case Dismissed," *Bozeman (MT) Avant Courier*, August 28, 1879.

159. "Attempted Jail Delivery," *Bozeman (MT) Weekly Chronicle*, May 14, 1884.

160. "Jail Delivery," *Bozeman (MT) Weekly Chronicle*, March 25, 1885.

161. *Bozeman (MT) Weekly Chronicle*, July 1, 1885.

162. "Broke Jail but Captured and Reincarcerated," *Weekly Avant Courier* (Bozeman, MT), July 14, 1894.

163. "Tunneled Their Way to Liberty," *Avant Courier* (Bozeman, MT), August 3, 1895.

164. "Cameron Is Captured," *Weekly Avant Courier* (Bozeman, MT), July 11, 1896.

165. "Jail Delivery," *Avant Courier* (Bozeman, MT), October 9, 1897.

166. *Avant Courier* (Bozeman, MT), May 8, 1903.

167. "Prisoners Make Their Escape," *Avant Courier* (Bozeman, MT), September 25, 1903.

168. *Republican-Courier* (Bozeman, MT), October 5, 1909.

169. "Sensational Jail Delivery Takes Place," *Evening Courier* (Bozeman, MT), December 22, 1911.

170. "Three More of the Escaped Prisoners Caught," *Republican-Courier* (Bozeman, MT), January 9, 1912.

171. "Prisoner Nearly Digs His Way Out of Jail" *Weekly Courier* (Bozeman, MT), May 28, 1913.

172. "Ross Maxwell Carried Steel Saws into Jail," *Weekly Courier* (Bozeman, MT), May 27, 1914.

173. "Prisoners Escape from County Jail," *Bozeman (MT) Courier*, December 13, 1929.

174. "Wilcox Tries to Break Jail," *Bozeman (MT) Chronicle*, September 21, 1933.

175. "Two Escape from Jail; $50 Each Offered," *Bozeman (MT) Daily Chronicle*, May 18, 1937.

176. "Laurent Taken in Hideout in Brush in Bridger Canyon," *Bozeman (MT) Chronicle*, May 23, 1937.

INDEX

ABOUT THE AUTHOR

*K*elly Hartman was raised in Silver Gate, Montana, attending kindergarten through eighth grade at the one-room schoolhouse in Cooke City. She received her AA in art at Northwest Community College in Powell, Wyoming, and her BFA in painting from Western Oregon University in Monmouth, Oregon. She started her museum career as the director of the Cooke City Montana Museum during its opening year. In 2016, she began work as the curator of the Gallatin History Museum in Bozeman, Montana. The museum is housed in the old county jail, where many of the prisoners in this book did time. Her books include *A Brief History of Cooke City* (2019), *Murder along the Yellowstone Trail: The Execution of Seth Danner* (2020), and *Murder and Mayhem in Gallatin County, Montana* (2021).

Visit us at
www.historypress.com

CPSIA information can be obtained
at www.ICGtesting.com
Printed in the USA
BVHW050944190522
637507BV00003B/101

9 781540 252456